I0153406

Navigating the Heart

Daily Steps for Courageous Relationship Growth

James R. Fleckenstein

Copyright © 2022 James R. Fleckenstein. All rights reserved. No portion of this book may be reproduced mechanically, electronically, or by any other means, including photocopying, without written permission from the publisher. It is illegal to copy this book, post it to a website, or distribute it by any other means without written permission from the publisher.

James R. Fleckenstein
The Earth Moved, LLC
8665 Sudley Road, #132
Manassas, Virginia 20110

jim@affirmativeintimacy.com
www.affirmativeintimacy.com

ISBN: 979-8-9860325-2-8

Introduction

Navigating the Heart: Daily Steps for Courageous Relationship Growth is a powerful tool. It will support you in learning and applying the principles of *Affirmative Intimacy®*.

Each quarter within *Navigating the Heart* corresponds to one of the Four Pillars of *Affirmative Intimacy®* - *Safe Space, Structured Dialog, Mindful Reason* and *Differentiation of Self*. Each of these principles is essential to creating and experiencing an optimal relationship. *Love That Works* offers worksheets and exercises (the "Hacks") to build your ability to implement the Pillars. *Navigating the Heart* is a tool for reflecting upon your day-to-day relationship experiences. I ask you to explore your feelings and your challenges as they come up. I invite you to take specific steps - in keeping with the principles - to address those challenges.

Navigating the Heart fosters a deliberative and reflective approach. I think this is an important adjunct to what you're doing with *Love That Works*. Even after you finish *Love That Works*, I invite you to continue using *Navigating the Heart*. Use it to keep applying the principles of *Affirmative Intimacy®* to your relationship – for the rest of your life.

As importantly, *Navigating the Heart* serves as an archive. It is a record of your thinking, planning and action. It becomes something you can refer to and reflect upon. Clients say that pausing for reflection - and appreciating their progress - is very helpful. This is especially true when you're discouraged. It's also helpful when you're confronted by a new challenge. It actually may be an old challenge in a slightly different form. Checking back may show how you overcame it before, and how to do it again.

Throughout *Navigating the Heart,* the emphasis is on recognizing success, however incremental. Success, not failure, is what motivates us. Obstacles and challenges are less frightening when we know we've overcome similar ones before, and have a plan to overcome these, too.

It is my heartfelt wish that *Navigating the Heart* provides you powerful support. Enjoy your journey of courageous relationship growth!

Using *Navigating the Heart*

Each week offers a quotation to inspire consideration of one or more aspects of the quarter's principle. At the beginning of each week, you have a few key questions to answer. These help set the tone for the week. I recommend doing it on a day when you have time to answer deliberately and thoughtfully.

First, capture your initial reaction to the quotation. This will show you where you are relative to the principle. A strong reaction is not a bad thing. But the strength and direction of your reaction sheds light on where your challenges may lie.

Next, reflect carefully upon how the situation or circumstance may show up in your life. It may not; this may just be an academic exercise. But if something hasn't yet come up, it typically will. So, work on it in good faith.

Next, I want you to focus on the positive changes you'd like to make this week. They may pertain to the quotation and your reaction, or they may not. Strong reactions typically lead to a realization that some changes may be in order.

Then reflect upon any challenges you may face on this topic or in making the changes you just identified. What (or who) might try to stop you? What (or who) might get in the way of your making the change?

Finally, think about the steps you'll take to overcome the challenges/obstacles. Making change requires a plan. This will prompt you to plan specific steps to keep yourself from being stopped cold.

After the weekly start page, you will see brief daily "check-ins." These allow you to touch on what's going on daily throughout the week. These can be handled in 10 or 15 minutes or less. The emphasis is on capturing successes. I want you to see and to congratulate yourself on your achievements and progress. This is important! It's easy to get discouraged when you don't feel you're making progress. Recognizing success is the best antidote to discouragement.

The second daily focus is identifying any specific things that have emerged that you want to work on and what you plan to do about them. Don't overthink this. Make quick notes; you can revisit them when you tackle next week's plan.

Finally, there's a weekly summary to capture your thoughts on how the week went and any particular observations you may have. It's just a quick summary, but it will be useful as a milestone/benchmark for yourself in the future. This may help you apply the same general techniques to overcome future obstacles.

Good luck, and happy journaling!

Quarter 1:
The First Pillar – *Safe Space*

Before anything else can work to improve your relationship, you must co-create *Safe Space*.

I found one thing that seemed missing in the work of relationship theorists. They never discussed what must come first before using any of their techniques. Unless you first create a favorable environment in which to use them, they're just ideas. It seemed that everyone simply assumed that everybody could just start right in using their ideas without first setting the stage in any way.

Interestingly, some of my insight about setting the stage before communicating even the most difficult news had also occurred to researchers in the medical/pharmaceutical field – both for patients and caregivers - and in education. But it doesn't seem to have made its way into the relationship counseling field.

So, I incorporated what I learned in these multiple disciplines to develop a method for creating *Safe Space*. Without *Safe Space*, you are seldom able to build an optimal relationship. Until *Safe Space* is co-created, the best techniques can fall on deaf ears. People simply won't take the risks necessary to achieve success if they don't feel safe sharing their truth. Therefore, *Safe Space* is the First Pillar of *Affirmative Intimacy*®

It is the foundational principle, the first step in making everything else work. If it's not safe to share *everything*, then it's not really safe to share *anything*, because you never know what's going to be triggering and derail the conversation. Before you can use any other technique to improve communication, process information appropriately, and grow intellectually, spiritually, and in relationship, you have to be operating from a place of safety.

When a man is penalized for honesty he learns to lie.

Stephan Labossiere (1978–) American certified relationship coach, speaker and author

My initial reaction to this quotation is:

_____
_____
_____

Does the behavior embodied in this quotation show up in my relationships and/or my life? If so, how?

_____
_____

What positive changes will I make this week to incorporate this new insight into my behavior?

_____
_____

What obstacles can I see to implementing these positive changes?

_____
_____

What is my plan for overcoming these obstacles?

_____
_____

Monday

How did it go today?   😞 😟 😐 🙂 😄

What successes did I enjoy today? *(Dig deep! Even small ones count, too!)*

_____

_____

What emerged/happened today that I want to work on, and what will I commit to doing?

_____

_____

Tuesday

How did it go today?   😞 😟 😐 🙂 😄

What successes did I enjoy today? *(Dig deep! Even small ones count, too!)*

_____

_____

What emerged/happened today that I want to work on, and what will I commit to doing?

_____

_____

Wednesday

How did it go today?   😞 😟 😐 🙂 😄

What successes did I enjoy today? *(Dig deep! Even small ones count, too!)*

_____

_____

What emerged/happened today that I want to work on, and what will I commit to doing?

_____

_____

Thursday

How did it go today?   😞 😟 😐 🙂 😄

What successes did I enjoy today? *(Dig deep! Even small ones count, too!)*

_____

_____

What emerged/happened today that I want to work on, and what will I commit to doing?

_____

_____

Friday

How did it go today? 😞 😟 😐 🙂 😄

What successes did I enjoy today? *(Dig deep! Even small ones count, too!)*

_____

_____

What emerged/happened today that I want to work on, and what will I commit to doing?

_____

_____

Saturday

How did it go today? 😞 😟 😐 🙂 😄

What successes did I enjoy today? *(Dig deep! Even small ones count, too!)*

_____

_____

What emerged/happened today that I want to work on, and what will I commit to doing?

_____

_____

Sunday

How did it go today? 😞 😟 😐 🙂 😄

What successes did I enjoy today? *(Dig deep! Even small ones count, too!)*

_____

_____

What emerged/happened today that I want to work on, and what will I commit to doing?

_____

_____

My week was:

_____

_____

_____

_____

_____

_____

Nothing other people do is because of you. It is because of themselves. All people live in their own dream, in their own mind; they are in a completely different world from the one we live in. When we take something personally, we make the assumption that they know what is in our world, and we try to impose our world on their world.

Don Miguel Ruiz (1952-) Mexican author

My initial reaction to this quotation is:

_____

_____

_____

Does the behavior embodied in this quotation show up in my relationships and/or my life? If so, how?

_____

_____

What positive changes will I make this week to incorporate this new insight into my behavior?

_____

_____

What obstacles can I see to implementing these positive changes?

_____

_____

What is my plan for overcoming these obstacles?

_____

_____

Monday

How did it go today?   😦 🙁 😐 🙂 😄

What successes did I enjoy today? *(Dig deep! Even small ones count, too!)*

_____

_____

What emerged/happened today that I want to work on, and what will I commit to doing?

_____

_____

Tuesday

How did it go today?   😦 🙁 😐 🙂 😄

What successes did I enjoy today? *(Dig deep! Even small ones count, too!)*

_____

_____

What emerged/happened today that I want to work on, and what will I commit to doing?

_____

_____

Wednesday

How did it go today?   😦 🙁 😐 🙂 😄

What successes did I enjoy today? *(Dig deep! Even small ones count, too!)*

_____

_____

What emerged/happened today that I want to work on, and what will I commit to doing?

_____

_____

Thursday

How did it go today?   😦 🙁 😐 🙂 😄

What successes did I enjoy today? *(Dig deep! Even small ones count, too!)*

_____

_____

What emerged/happened today that I want to work on, and what will I commit to doing?

_____

_____

Friday

How did it go today? 😞 😞 😐 🙂 😄

What successes did I enjoy today? *(Dig deep! Even small ones count, too!)*

_____

_____

What emerged/happened today that I want to work on, and what will I commit to doing?

_____

_____

Saturday

How did it go today? 😞 😞 😐 🙂 😄

What successes did I enjoy today? *(Dig deep! Even small ones count, too!)*

_____

_____

What emerged/happened today that I want to work on, and what will I commit to doing?

_____

_____

Sunday

How did it go today? 😞 😞 😐 🙂 😄

What successes did I enjoy today? *(Dig deep! Even small ones count, too!)*

_____

_____

What emerged/happened today that I want to work on, and what will I commit to doing?

_____

_____

My week was:

_____

_____

_____

_____

_____

_____

_____

WEEK 3

I love you, and because I love you, I would sooner have you hate me for telling you the truth than adore me for telling you lies.

Pietro Aretino (1492-1556) Italian poet, writer, and dramatist

My initial reaction to this quotation is:

_____

_____

_____

Does the behavior embodied in this quotation show up in my relationships and/or my life? If so, how?

_____

_____

What positive changes will I make this week to incorporate this new insight into my behavior?

_____

_____

What obstacles can I see to implementing these positive changes?

_____

_____

What is my plan for overcoming these obstacles?

_____

_____

Monday

How did it go today? 😟 😞 😐 🙂 😄

What successes did I enjoy today? *(Dig deep! Even small ones count, too!)*

_____

_____

What emerged/happened today that I want to work on, and what will I commit to doing?

_____

_____

Tuesday

How did it go today? 😟 😞 😐 🙂 😄

What successes did I enjoy today? *(Dig deep! Even small ones count, too!)*

_____

_____

What emerged/happened today that I want to work on, and what will I commit to doing?

_____

_____

Wednesday

How did it go today? 😟 😞 😐 🙂 😄

What successes did I enjoy today? *(Dig deep! Even small ones count, too!)*

_____

_____

What emerged/happened today that I want to work on, and what will I commit to doing?

_____

_____

Thursday

How did it go today? 😟 😞 😐 🙂 😄

What successes did I enjoy today? *(Dig deep! Even small ones count, too!)*

_____

_____

What emerged/happened today that I want to work on, and what will I commit to doing?

_____

_____

Friday

How did it go today? 😦 😦 😐 😊 😄

What successes did I enjoy today? *(Dig deep! Even small ones count, too!)*

_____

_____

What emerged/happened today that I want to work on, and what will I commit to doing?

_____

_____

Saturday

How did it go today? 😦 😦 😐 😊 😄

What successes did I enjoy today? *(Dig deep! Even small ones count, too!)*

_____

_____

What emerged/happened today that I want to work on, and what will I commit to doing?

_____

_____

Sunday

How did it go today? 😦 😦 😐 😊 😄

What successes did I enjoy today? *(Dig deep! Even small ones count, too!)*

_____

_____

What emerged/happened today that I want to work on, and what will I commit to doing?

_____

_____

My week was:

_____

_____

_____

_____

_____

_____

Speak when you are angry and you will make the best speech you will ever regret.

Ambrose Bierce (1842-1914) American editorialist, journalist, short-story writer, fabulist, and satirist

My initial reaction to this quotation is:

_____

_____

_____

Does the behavior embodied in this quotation show up in my relationships and/or my life? If so, how?

_____

_____

What positive changes will I make this week to incorporate this new insight into my behavior?

_____

_____

What obstacles can I see to implementing these positive changes?

_____

_____

What is my plan for overcoming these obstacles?

_____

_____

Monday

How did it go today? 🙁 🙁 😐 🙂 😃

What successes did I enjoy today? *(Dig deep! Even small ones count, too!)*

_____

_____

What emerged/happened today that I want to work on, and what will I commit to doing?

_____

Tuesday

How did it go today? 🙁 🙁 😐 🙂 😃

What successes did I enjoy today? *(Dig deep! Even small ones count, too!)*

_____

_____

What emerged/happened today that I want to work on, and what will I commit to doing?

_____

_____

Wednesday

How did it go today? 😢 🙁 😐 🙂 😃

What successes did I enjoy today? *(Dig deep! Even small ones count, too!)*

_____

_____

What emerged/happened today that I want to work on, and what will I commit to doing?

_____

_____

Thursday

How did it go today? 🙁 🙁 😐 🙂 😃

What successes did I enjoy today? *(Dig deep! Even small ones count, too!)*

_____

_____

What emerged/happened today that I want to work on, and what will I commit to doing?

_____

_____

Friday

How did it go today? 😞 😟 😐 🙂 😄

What successes did I enjoy today? *(Dig deep! Even small ones count, too!)*

_____

_____

What emerged/happened today that I want to work on, and what will I commit to doing?

_____

_____

Saturday

How did it go today? 😞 😟 😐 🙂 😄

What successes did I enjoy today? *(Dig deep! Even small ones count, too!)*

_____

_____

What emerged/happened today that I want to work on, and what will I commit to doing?

_____

_____

Sunday

How did it go today? 😞 😟 😐 🙂 😄

What successes did I enjoy today? *(Dig deep! Even small ones count, too!)*

_____

_____

What emerged/happened today that I want to work on, and what will I commit to doing?

_____

_____

My week was:

_____

_____

_____

_____

_____

_____

WEEK 5

We know from our experience that it is easier to develop trust in another person...if we believe that we can disagree, and we will not be abandoned or hurt for our differences. It is difficult to trust those who deny us the right to be ourselves.

Susan Wheelan, Ph.D. (?) American psychologist, professor and author

My initial reaction to this quotation is:

_____
_____
_____

Does the behavior embodied in this quotation show up in my relationships and/or my life? If so, how?

_____
_____

What positive changes will I make this week to incorporate this new insight into my behavior?

_____
_____

What obstacles can I see to implementing these positive changes?

_____
_____

What is my plan for overcoming these obstacles?

_____
_____

Monday

How did it go today?   🙁 🙁 😐 🙂 😀

What successes did I enjoy today? *(Dig deep! Even small ones count, too!)*

_____

_____

What emerged/happened today that I want to work on, and what will I commit to doing?

_____

_____

Tuesday

How did it go today?   🙁 🙁 😐 🙂 😀

What successes did I enjoy today? *(Dig deep! Even small ones count, too!)*

_____

_____

What emerged/happened today that I want to work on, and what will I commit to doing?

_____

_____

Wednesday

How did it go today?   🙁 🙁 😐 🙂 😀

What successes did I enjoy today? *(Dig deep! Even small ones count, too!)*

_____

_____

What emerged/happened today that I want to work on, and what will I commit to doing?

_____

_____

Thursday

How did it go today?   🙁 🙁 😐 🙂 😀

What successes did I enjoy today? *(Dig deep! Even small ones count, too!)*

_____

_____

What emerged/happened today that I want to work on, and what will I commit to doing?

_____

_____

Friday

How did it go today?   🙁 🙁 😐 🙂 😃

What successes did I enjoy today? *(Dig deep! Even small ones count, too!)*

_____

_____

What emerged/happened today that I want to work on, and what will I commit to doing?

_____

_____

Saturday

How did it go today?   🙁 🙁 😐 🙂 😃

What successes did I enjoy today? *(Dig deep! Even small ones count, too!)*

_____

_____

What emerged/happened today that I want to work on, and what will I commit to doing?

_____

_____

Sunday

How did it go today?   🙁 🙁 😐 🙂 😃

What successes did I enjoy today? *(Dig deep! Even small ones count, too!)*

_____

_____

What emerged/happened today that I want to work on, and what will I commit to doing?

_____

_____

My week was:

_____

_____

_____

_____

_____

_____

The use of tact is always needful but it is especially necessary when speaking a truth that may strike a sensitive nerve in another.

Robert E. Fisher (1940–) American author and historian

My initial reaction to this quotation is:

_____

_____

_____

Does the behavior embodied in this quotation show up in my relationships and/or my life? If so, how?

_____

_____

What positive changes will I make this week to incorporate this new insight into my behavior?

_____

_____

What obstacles can I see to implementing these positive changes?

_____

_____

What is my plan for overcoming these obstacles?

_____

_____

Monday

How did it go today? :(:(:| :) :D

What successes did I enjoy today? *(Dig deep! Even small ones count, too!)*

_____

_____

What emerged/happened today that I want to work on, and what will I commit to doing?

_____

_____

Tuesday

How did it go today? :(:(:| :) :D

What successes did I enjoy today? *(Dig deep! Even small ones count, too!)*

_____

_____

What emerged/happened today that I want to work on, and what will I commit to doing?

_____

_____

Wednesday

How did it go today? :(:(:| :) :D

What successes did I enjoy today? *(Dig deep! Even small ones count, too!)*

_____

_____

What emerged/happened today that I want to work on, and what will I commit to doing?

_____

_____

Thursday

How did it go today? :(:(:| :) :D

What successes did I enjoy today? *(Dig deep! Even small ones count, too!)*

_____

_____

What emerged/happened today that I want to work on, and what will I commit to doing?

_____

_____

Friday

How did it go today?   😟 😦 😐 🙂 😃

What successes did I enjoy today? *(Dig deep! Even small ones count, too!)*

_____

_____

What emerged/happened today that I want to work on, and what will I commit to doing?

_____

_____

Saturday

How did it go today?   😟 😦 😐 🙂 😃

What successes did I enjoy today? *(Dig deep! Even small ones count, too!)*

_____

_____

What emerged/happened today that I want to work on, and what will I commit to doing?

_____

_____

Sunday

How did it go today?   😟 😦 😐 🙂 😃

What successes did I enjoy today? *(Dig deep! Even small ones count, too!)*

_____

_____

What emerged/happened today that I want to work on, and what will I commit to doing?

_____

_____

My week was:

_____

_____

_____

_____

_____

_____

WEEK 7

Fear is not in the habit of speaking truth; when perfect sincerity is expected, perfect freedom must be allowed; nor has anyone who is apt to be angry when he hears the truth any cause to wonder that he does not hear it.

Tacitus (56–117 CE) Roman senator and historian

My initial reaction to this quotation is:

_____
_____
_____

Does the behavior embodied in this quotation show up in my relationships and/or my life? If so, how?

_____
_____

What positive changes will I make this week to incorporate this new insight into my behavior?

_____
_____

What obstacles can I see to implementing these positive changes?

_____
_____

What is my plan for overcoming these obstacles?

_____
_____

Monday

How did it go today? 😞 😞 😐 🙂 😃

What successes did I enjoy today? *(Dig deep! Even small ones count, too!)*

_____

_____

What emerged/happened today that I want to work on, and what will I commit to doing?

_____

_____

Tuesday

How did it go today? 😞 😞 😐 🙂 😃

What successes did I enjoy today? *(Dig deep! Even small ones count, too!)*

_____

_____

What emerged/happened today that I want to work on, and what will I commit to doing?

_____

_____

Wednesday

How did it go today? 😞 😞 😐 🙂 😃

What successes did I enjoy today? *(Dig deep! Even small ones count, too!)*

_____

_____

What emerged/happened today that I want to work on, and what will I commit to doing?

_____

_____

Thursday

How did it go today? 😞 😞 😐 🙂 😃

What successes did I enjoy today? *(Dig deep! Even small ones count, too!)*

_____

_____

What emerged/happened today that I want to work on, and what will I commit to doing?

_____

_____

Friday

How did it go today?

What successes did I enjoy today? *(Dig deep! Even small ones count, too!)*

_____

_____

What emerged/happened today that I want to work on, and what will I commit to doing?

_____

_____

Saturday

How did it go today?

What successes did I enjoy today? *(Dig deep! Even small ones count, too!)*

_____

_____

What emerged/happened today that I want to work on, and what will I commit to doing?

_____

_____

Sunday

How did it go today?

What successes did I enjoy today? *(Dig deep! Even small ones count, too!)*

_____

_____

What emerged/happened today that I want to work on, and what will I commit to doing?

_____

_____

My week was:

_____

_____

_____

_____

_____

_____

WEEK 8

> In order that all men may be taught to speak the truth, it is necessary that all likewise should learn to hear it.
>
> *Samuel Johnson (1709-1784) English poet, essayist, moralist, literary critic, biographer, editor and lexicographer*

My initial reaction to this quotation is:

_____

_____

_____

Does the behavior embodied in this quotation show up in my relationships and/or my life? If so, how?

_____

_____

What positive changes will I make this week to incorporate this new insight into my behavior?

_____

_____

What obstacles can I see to implementing these positive changes?

_____

_____

What is my plan for overcoming these obstacles?

_____

_____

Monday

How did it go today?   ☹ ☹ 😐 🙂 😄

What successes did I enjoy today? *(Dig deep! Even small ones count, too!)*

_____

_____

What emerged/happened today that I want to work on, and what will I commit to doing?

_____

_____

Tuesday

How did it go today?   ☹ ☹ 😐 🙂 😄

What successes did I enjoy today? *(Dig deep! Even small ones count, too!)*

_____

_____

What emerged/happened today that I want to work on, and what will I commit to doing?

_____

_____

Wednesday

How did it go today?   ☹ ☹ 😐 🙂 😄

What successes did I enjoy today? *(Dig deep! Even small ones count, too!)*

_____

_____

What emerged/happened today that I want to work on, and what will I commit to doing?

_____

_____

Thursday

How did it go today?   ☹ ☹ 😐 🙂 😄

What successes did I enjoy today? *(Dig deep! Even small ones count, too!)*

_____

_____

What emerged/happened today that I want to work on, and what will I commit to doing?

_____

_____

Friday

How did it go today?

What successes did I enjoy today? *(Dig deep! Even small ones count, too!)*

_____

_____

What emerged/happened today that I want to work on, and what will I commit to doing?

_____

_____

Saturday

How did it go today?

What successes did I enjoy today? *(Dig deep! Even small ones count, too!)*

_____

_____

What emerged/happened today that I want to work on, and what will I commit to doing?

_____

_____

Sunday

How did it go today?

What successes did I enjoy today? *(Dig deep! Even small ones count, too!)*

_____

_____

What emerged/happened today that I want to work on, and what will I commit to doing?

_____

_____

My week was:

_____

_____

_____

_____

_____

_____

_____

WEEK 9

More information is always better than less. When people know the reason things are happening, even if it's bad news, they can adjust their expectations and react accordingly. Keeping people in the dark only serves to stir negative emotions.

Simon Sinek (1973–) English author and leadership expert

My initial reaction to this quotation is:

_____

_____

_____

Does the behavior embodied in this quotation show up in my relationships and/or my life? If so, how?

_____

_____

What positive changes will I make this week to incorporate this new insight into my behavior?

_____

_____

What obstacles can I see to implementing these positive changes?

_____

_____

What is my plan for overcoming these obstacles?

_____

_____

Monday

How did it go today?　　😟　☹️　😐　🙂　😀

What successes did I enjoy today? *(Dig deep! Even small ones count, too!)*

_____

_____

What emerged/happened today that I want to work on, and what will I commit to doing?

_____

_____

Tuesday

How did it go today?　　😟　☹️　😐　🙂　😀

What successes did I enjoy today? *(Dig deep! Even small ones count, too!)*

_____

_____

What emerged/happened today that I want to work on, and what will I commit to doing?

_____

_____

Wednesday

How did it go today?　　😟　☹️　😐　🙂　😀

What successes did I enjoy today? *(Dig deep! Even small ones count, too!)*

_____

_____

What emerged/happened today that I want to work on, and what will I commit to doing?

_____

_____

Thursday

How did it go today?　　😟　☹️　😐　🙂　😀

What successes did I enjoy today? *(Dig deep! Even small ones count, too!)*

_____

_____

What emerged/happened today that I want to work on, and what will I commit to doing?

_____

_____

Friday

How did it go today? 😞 😟 😐 🙂 😀

What successes did I enjoy today? *(Dig deep! Even small ones count, too!)*

_____

_____

What emerged/happened today that I want to work on, and what will I commit to doing?

_____

_____

Saturday

How did it go today? 😞 😟 😐 🙂 😀

What successes did I enjoy today? *(Dig deep! Even small ones count, too!)*

_____

_____

What emerged/happened today that I want to work on, and what will I commit to doing?

_____

_____

Sunday

How did it go today? 😞 😟 😐 🙂 😀

What successes did I enjoy today? *(Dig deep! Even small ones count, too!)*

_____

_____

What emerged/happened today that I want to work on, and what will I commit to doing?

_____

_____

My week was:

_____

_____

_____

_____

_____

_____

WEEK 10

When we speak we are afraid our words will not be heard or welcomed. But when we are silent, we are still afraid. So it is better to speak.

Audre Lorde (1934-1992) Caribbean-American writer, radical feminist, womanist, lesbian, and civil rights activist

My initial reaction to this quotation is:

_____

_____

_____

Does the behavior embodied in this quotation show up in my relationships and/or my life? If so, how?

_____

_____

What positive changes will I make this week to incorporate this new insight into my behavior?

_____

_____

What obstacles can I see to implementing these positive changes?

_____

_____

What is my plan for overcoming these obstacles?

_____

_____

Monday

How did it go today? ☹ 🙁 😐 🙂 😃

What successes did I enjoy today? *(Dig deep! Even small ones count, too!)*

_____

_____

What emerged/happened today that I want to work on, and what will I commit to doing?

_____

_____

Tuesday

How did it go today? ☹ 🙁 😐 🙂 😃

What successes did I enjoy today? *(Dig deep! Even small ones count, too!)*

_____

_____

What emerged/happened today that I want to work on, and what will I commit to doing?

_____

_____

Wednesday

How did it go today? ☹ 🙁 😐 🙂 😃

What successes did I enjoy today? *(Dig deep! Even small ones count, too!)*

_____

_____

What emerged/happened today that I want to work on, and what will I commit to doing?

_____

_____

Thursday

How did it go today? ☹ 🙁 😐 🙂 😃

What successes did I enjoy today? *(Dig deep! Even small ones count, too!)*

_____

_____

What emerged/happened today that I want to work on, and what will I commit to doing?

_____

_____

Friday

How did it go today? 🙁 🙁 😐 🙂 😃

What successes did I enjoy today? *(Dig deep! Even small ones count, too!)*

_____

_____

What emerged/happened today that I want to work on, and what will I commit to doing?

_____

_____

Saturday

How did it go today? 🙁 🙁 😐 🙂 😃

What successes did I enjoy today? *(Dig deep! Even small ones count, too!)*

_____

_____

What emerged/happened today that I want to work on, and what will I commit to doing?

_____

_____

Sunday

How did it go today? 🙁 🙁 😐 🙂 😃

What successes did I enjoy today? *(Dig deep! Even small ones count, too!)*

_____

_____

What emerged/happened today that I want to work on, and what will I commit to doing?

_____

_____

My week was:

_____

_____

_____

_____

_____

_____

WEEK 11

The one charm about marriage is that it makes a life of deception absolutely necessary for both parties.

Oscar Wilde (1854-1900) Irish playwright, novelist, and poet

My initial reaction to this quotation is:

_____

_____

_____

Does the behavior embodied in this quotation show up in my relationships and/or my life? If so, how?

_____

_____

What positive changes will I make this week to incorporate this new insight into my behavior?

_____

_____

What obstacles can I see to implementing these positive changes?

_____

_____

What is my plan for overcoming these obstacles?

_____

_____

Monday

How did it go today? ☹ ☹ 😐 🙂 😃

What successes did I enjoy today? *(Dig deep! Even small ones count, too!)*

_____

_____

What emerged/happened today that I want to work on, and what will I commit to doing?

_____

_____

Tuesday

How did it go today? ☹ ☹ 😐 🙂 😃

What successes did I enjoy today? *(Dig deep! Even small ones count, too!)*

_____

_____

What emerged/happened today that I want to work on, and what will I commit to doing?

_____

_____

Wednesday

How did it go today? ☹ ☹ 😐 🙂 😃

What successes did I enjoy today? *(Dig deep! Even small ones count, too!)*

_____

_____

What emerged/happened today that I want to work on, and what will I commit to doing?

_____

_____

Thursday

How did it go today? ☹ ☹ 😐 🙂 😃

What successes did I enjoy today? *(Dig deep! Even small ones count, too!)*

_____

_____

What emerged/happened today that I want to work on, and what will I commit to doing?

_____

_____

Friday

How did it go today?

What successes did I enjoy today? *(Dig deep! Even small ones count, too!)*

_____

_____

What emerged/happened today that I want to work on, and what will I commit to doing?

_____

_____

Saturday

How did it go today?

What successes did I enjoy today? *(Dig deep! Even small ones count, too!)*

_____

_____

What emerged/happened today that I want to work on, and what will I commit to doing?

_____

_____

Sunday

How did it go today?

What successes did I enjoy today? *(Dig deep! Even small ones count, too!)*

_____

_____

What emerged/happened today that I want to work on, and what will I commit to doing?

_____

_____

My week was:

_____

_____

_____

_____

_____

Sometimes people fear the truth. They'd rather not speak to you than know what you really think.

Paloma Faith (1981–) English singer and actress

My initial reaction to this quotation is:

_____

_____

_____

Does the behavior embodied in this quotation show up in my relationships and/or my life? If so, how?

_____

_____

What positive changes will I make this week to incorporate this new insight into my behavior?

_____

_____

What obstacles can I see to implementing these positive changes?

_____

_____

What is my plan for overcoming these obstacles?

_____

_____

Monday

How did it go today?   😦 😦 😐 🙂 😀

What successes did I enjoy today? *(Dig deep! Even small ones count, too!)*

_____

_____

What emerged/happened today that I want to work on, and what will I commit to doing?

_____

_____

Tuesday

How did it go today?   😦 😦 😐 🙂 😀

What successes did I enjoy today? *(Dig deep! Even small ones count, too!)*

_____

_____

What emerged/happened today that I want to work on, and what will I commit to doing?

_____

_____

Wednesday

How did it go today?   😦 😦 😐 🙂 😀

What successes did I enjoy today? *(Dig deep! Even small ones count, too!)*

_____

_____

What emerged/happened today that I want to work on, and what will I commit to doing?

_____

_____

Thursday

How did it go today?   😦 😦 😐 🙂 😀

What successes did I enjoy today? *(Dig deep! Even small ones count, too!)*

_____

_____

What emerged/happened today that I want to work on, and what will I commit to doing?

_____

_____

Friday

How did it go today? 😦 😟 😐 🙂 😄

What successes did I enjoy today? *(Dig deep! Even small ones count, too!)*

_____

_____

What emerged/happened today that I want to work on, and what will I commit to doing?

_____

_____

Saturday

How did it go today? 😦 😟 😐 🙂 😄

What successes did I enjoy today? *(Dig deep! Even small ones count, too!)*

_____

_____

What emerged/happened today that I want to work on, and what will I commit to doing?

_____

_____

Sunday

How did it go today? 😦 😟 😐 🙂 😄

What successes did I enjoy today? *(Dig deep! Even small ones count, too!)*

_____

_____

What emerged/happened today that I want to work on, and what will I commit to doing?

_____

_____

My week was:

_____

_____

_____

_____

_____

_____

Only enemies speak the truth;
friends and lovers lie endlessly,
caught in the web of duty.

Stephen King (1947–) American author

My initial reaction to this quotation is:

_____
_____
_____

Does the behavior embodied in this quotation show up in my relationships and/or my life? If so, how?

_____
_____

What positive changes will I make this week to incorporate this new insight into my behavior?

_____
_____

What obstacles can I see to implementing these positive changes?

_____
_____

What is my plan for overcoming these obstacles?

_____
_____

Monday

How did it go today?   🙁 🙁 😐 🙂 😀

What successes did I enjoy today? *(Dig deep! Even small ones count, too!)*

_____

_____

What emerged/happened today that I want to work on, and what will I commit to doing?

_____

_____

Tuesday

How did it go today?   🙁 🙁 😐 🙂 😀

What successes did I enjoy today? *(Dig deep! Even small ones count, too!)*

_____

_____

What emerged/happened today that I want to work on, and what will I commit to doing?

_____

_____

Wednesday

How did it go today?   🙁 🙁 😐 🙂 😀

What successes did I enjoy today? *(Dig deep! Even small ones count, too!)*

_____

_____

What emerged/happened today that I want to work on, and what will I commit to doing?

_____

_____

Thursday

How did it go today?   🙁 🙁 😐 🙂 😀

What successes did I enjoy today? *(Dig deep! Even small ones count, too!)*

_____

_____

What emerged/happened today that I want to work on, and what will I commit to doing?

_____

_____

Friday

How did it go today? 😦 😧 😐 🙂 😃

What successes did I enjoy today? *(Dig deep! Even small ones count, too!)*

_____

_____

What emerged/happened today that I want to work on, and what will I commit to doing?

_____

_____

Saturday

How did it go today? 😦 😧 😐 🙂 😃

What successes did I enjoy today? *(Dig deep! Even small ones count, too!)*

_____

_____

What emerged/happened today that I want to work on, and what will I commit to doing?

_____

_____

Sunday

How did it go today? 😦 😧 😐 🙂 😃

What successes did I enjoy today? *(Dig deep! Even small ones count, too!)*

_____

_____

What emerged/happened today that I want to work on, and what will I commit to doing?

_____

_____

My week was:

_____

_____

_____

_____

_____

_____

Quarter 2:
The Second Pillar – *Structured Dialog*

The *way* you choose to communicate can do much to determine whether your communication succeeds or fails.

Communication is a critical skill in every method of personal and relationship growth I studied. It's also one of the most frequent trouble spots reported by individuals and counselors alike. I *had* to include communication education. Though based in part on the work of psychologist Harville Hendrix, I also blended in important insights from many other specialists in difficult interpersonal communications.

Fortunately, there is a great deal of research on how best to communicate, and the many reasons why we so often fail to communicate well. My task in creating the *Structured Dialog* Pillar of *Affirmative Intimacy*® was to put together a streamlined, effective approach that fit in with and enhanced the other Pillars.

After you've co-created *Safe Space* in which to operate, you must devote your energies to being sure you are communicating effectively. The *Structured Dialog* process seems terribly cumbersome and awkward at first. You're compelled to spend a lot of mental energy on the process itself in the early stages. But once you begin to master the concept, two important things happen. First, the process becomes less awkward and more natural. Second, the rewards become increasingly obvious and are a strong source of positive reinforcement.

Over time, you'll be so used to the process that you'll gain the ability to use shortcuts with each other that achieve the same results. If something really becomes a sticking point for your communication, you may have to revert to the detailed, step-by-step approach to get past it, but such instances should become increasingly rare.

Clear and accurate communication between partners helps set the stage for applying the next Pillar, *Mindful Reason.*

WEEK 14

When we name things correctly, we comprehend them correctly, without adding information or judgments that aren't there. Does someone bathe quickly? Don't say he bathes poorly, but quickly. Name the situation as it is, don't filter it through your judgments.

Epictetus (55-135 CE) A Greek-speaking Stoic philosopher

My initial reaction to this quotation is:

_____

_____

_____

Does the behavior embodied in this quotation show up in my relationships and/or my life? If so, how?

_____

_____

What positive changes will I make this week to incorporate this new insight into my behavior?

_____

_____

What obstacles can I see to implementing these positive changes?

_____

_____

What is my plan for overcoming these obstacles?

_____

_____

Monday

How did it go today?　　😟　😦　😐　🙂　😀

What successes did I enjoy today? *(Dig deep! Even small ones count, too!)*

_____

_____

What emerged/happened today that I want to work on, and what will I commit to doing?

_____

_____

Tuesday

How did it go today?　　😟　😦　😐　🙂　😀

What successes did I enjoy today? *(Dig deep! Even small ones count, too!)*

_____

_____

What emerged/happened today that I want to work on, and what will I commit to doing?

_____

_____

Wednesday

How did it go today?　　😟　😦　😐　🙂　😀

What successes did I enjoy today? *(Dig deep! Even small ones count, too!)*

_____

_____

What emerged/happened today that I want to work on, and what will I commit to doing?

_____

_____

Thursday

How did it go today?　　😟　😦　😐　🙂　😀

What successes did I enjoy today? *(Dig deep! Even small ones count, too!)*

_____

_____

What emerged/happened today that I want to work on, and what will I commit to doing?

_____

_____

Friday

How did it go today?

What successes did I enjoy today? *(Dig deep! Even small ones count, too!)*

_____

_____

What emerged/happened today that I want to work on, and what will I commit to doing?

_____

_____

Saturday

How did it go today?

What successes did I enjoy today? *(Dig deep! Even small ones count, too!)*

_____

_____

What emerged/happened today that I want to work on, and what will I commit to doing?

_____

_____

Sunday

How did it go today?

What successes did I enjoy today? *(Dig deep! Even small ones count, too!)*

_____

_____

What emerged/happened today that I want to work on, and what will I commit to doing?

_____

_____

My week was:

_____

_____

_____

_____

_____

Discussion is an exchange of knowledge; argument an exchange of ignorance.

Robert Quillen (1887-1948) American journalist and humorist

My initial reaction to this quotation is:

_____

_____

_____

Does the behavior embodied in this quotation show up in my relationships and/or my life? If so, how?

_____

_____

What positive changes will I make this week to incorporate this new insight into my behavior?

_____

_____

What obstacles can I see to implementing these positive changes?

_____

_____

What is my plan for overcoming these obstacles?

_____

_____

Monday

How did it go today?   🙁 😟 😐 🙂 😃

What successes did I enjoy today? *(Dig deep! Even small ones count, too!)*

_____

_____

What emerged/happened today that I want to work on, and what will I commit to doing?

_____

_____

Tuesday

How did it go today?   🙁 😟 😐 🙂 😃

What successes did I enjoy today? *(Dig deep! Even small ones count, too!)*

_____

_____

What emerged/happened today that I want to work on, and what will I commit to doing?

_____

_____

Wednesday

How did it go today?   🙁 😟 😐 🙂 😃

What successes did I enjoy today? *(Dig deep! Even small ones count, too!)*

_____

_____

What emerged/happened today that I want to work on, and what will I commit to doing?

_____

_____

Thursday

How did it go today?   🙁 😟 😐 🙂 😃

What successes did I enjoy today? *(Dig deep! Even small ones count, too!)*

_____

_____

What emerged/happened today that I want to work on, and what will I commit to doing?

_____

_____

Friday

How did it go today?

What successes did I enjoy today? *(Dig deep! Even small ones count, too!)*

_____

_____

What emerged/happened today that I want to work on, and what will I commit to doing?

_____

_____

Saturday

How did it go today?

What successes did I enjoy today? *(Dig deep! Even small ones count, too!)*

_____

_____

What emerged/happened today that I want to work on, and what will I commit to doing?

_____

_____

Sunday

How did it go today?

What successes did I enjoy today? *(Dig deep! Even small ones count, too!)*

_____

_____

What emerged/happened today that I want to work on, and what will I commit to doing?

_____

_____

My week was:

_____

_____

_____

_____

_____

_____

Two monologues do not make a dialogue.

Jeff Daly (?) American architect, exhibit designer and museum consultant

My initial reaction to this quotation is:

_____

_____

_____

Does the behavior embodied in this quotation show up in my relationships and/or my life? If so, how?

_____

_____

What positive changes will I make this week to incorporate this new insight into my behavior?

_____

_____

What obstacles can I see to implementing these positive changes?

_____

_____

What is my plan for overcoming these obstacles?

_____

_____

Monday

How did it go today?   😟 😦 😐 🙂 😀

What successes did I enjoy today? *(Dig deep! Even small ones count, too!)*

_____

_____

What emerged/happened today that I want to work on, and what will I commit to doing?

_____

_____

Tuesday

How did it go today?   😟 😦 😐 🙂 😀

What successes did I enjoy today? *(Dig deep! Even small ones count, too!)*

_____

_____

What emerged/happened today that I want to work on, and what will I commit to doing?

_____

_____

Wednesday

How did it go today?   😟 😦 😐 🙂 😀

What successes did I enjoy today? *(Dig deep! Even small ones count, too!)*

_____

_____

What emerged/happened today that I want to work on, and what will I commit to doing?

_____

_____

Thursday

How did it go today?   😟 😦 😐 🙂 😀

What successes did I enjoy today? *(Dig deep! Even small ones count, too!)*

_____

_____

What emerged/happened today that I want to work on, and what will I commit to doing?

_____

_____

Friday

How did it go today?

What successes did I enjoy today? *(Dig deep! Even small ones count, too!)*

_____

_____

What emerged/happened today that I want to work on, and what will I commit to doing?

_____

_____

Saturday

How did it go today?

What successes did I enjoy today? *(Dig deep! Even small ones count, too!)*

_____

_____

What emerged/happened today that I want to work on, and what will I commit to doing?

_____

_____

Sunday

How did it go today?

What successes did I enjoy today? *(Dig deep! Even small ones count, too!)*

_____

_____

What emerged/happened today that I want to work on, and what will I commit to doing?

_____

_____

My week was:

_____

_____

_____

_____

_____

_____

The single biggest problem in communication is the illusion that it has taken place.

George Bernard Shaw (1856-1950) Nobel Prize-winning Irish playwright and critic

My initial reaction to this quotation is:

_____

_____

_____

Does the behavior embodied in this quotation show up in my relationships and/or my life? If so, how?

_____

_____

What positive changes will I make this week to incorporate this new insight into my behavior?

_____

_____

What obstacles can I see to implementing these positive changes?

_____

_____

What is my plan for overcoming these obstacles?

_____

_____

Monday

How did it go today?　　☹　☹　😐　🙂　😀

What successes did I enjoy today? *(Dig deep! Even small ones count, too!)*

_____

_____

What emerged/happened today that I want to work on, and what will I commit to doing?

_____

_____

Tuesday

How did it go today?　　☹　☹　😐　🙂　😀

What successes did I enjoy today? *(Dig deep! Even small ones count, too!)*

_____

_____

What emerged/happened today that I want to work on, and what will I commit to doing?

_____

_____

Wednesday

How did it go today?　　☹　☹　😐　🙂　😀

What successes did I enjoy today? *(Dig deep! Even small ones count, too!)*

_____

_____

What emerged/happened today that I want to work on, and what will I commit to doing?

_____

_____

Thursday

How did it go today?　　☹　☹　😐　🙂　😀

What successes did I enjoy today? *(Dig deep! Even small ones count, too!)*

_____

_____

What emerged/happened today that I want to work on, and what will I commit to doing?

_____

_____

Friday

How did it go today?   😦 😦 😐 🙂 😄

What successes did I enjoy today? *(Dig deep! Even small ones count, too!)*

_____

_____

What emerged/happened today that I want to work on, and what will I commit to doing?

_____

_____

Saturday

How did it go today?   😦 😦 😐 🙂 😄

What successes did I enjoy today? *(Dig deep! Even small ones count, too!)*

_____

_____

What emerged/happened today that I want to work on, and what will I commit to doing?

_____

_____

Sunday

How did it go today?   😦 😦 😐 🙂 😄

What successes did I enjoy today? *(Dig deep! Even small ones count, too!)*

_____

_____

What emerged/happened today that I want to work on, and what will I commit to doing?

_____

_____

My week was:

_____

_____

_____

_____

_____

_____

WEEK 18

If you understood everything I said, you'd *be* me.

Miles Davis (1926-1991) American jazz musician, trumpeter, bandleader, and composer

My initial reaction to this quotation is:

_____
_____
_____

Does the behavior embodied in this quotation show up in my relationships and/or my life? If so, how?

_____
_____

What positive changes will I make this week to incorporate this new insight into my behavior?

_____
_____

What obstacles can I see to implementing these positive changes?

_____
_____

What is my plan for overcoming these obstacles?

_____
_____

Monday

How did it go today? 😟 😦 😐 🙂 😃

What successes did I enjoy today? *(Dig deep! Even small ones count, too!)*

_____

_____

What emerged/happened today that I want to work on, and what will I commit to doing?

_____

_____

Tuesday

How did it go today? 😟 😦 😐 🙂 😃

What successes did I enjoy today? *(Dig deep! Even small ones count, too!)*

_____

_____

What emerged/happened today that I want to work on, and what will I commit to doing?

_____

_____

Wednesday

How did it go today? 😟 😦 😐 🙂 😃

What successes did I enjoy today? *(Dig deep! Even small ones count, too!)*

_____

_____

What emerged/happened today that I want to work on, and what will I commit to doing?

_____

_____

Thursday

How did it go today? 😟 😦 😐 🙂 😃

What successes did I enjoy today? *(Dig deep! Even small ones count, too!)*

_____

_____

What emerged/happened today that I want to work on, and what will I commit to doing?

_____

_____

Friday

How did it go today?   😕   😦   😐   🙂   😃

What successes did I enjoy today? *(Dig deep! Even small ones count, too!)*

_____

_____

What emerged/happened today that I want to work on, and what will I commit to doing?

_____

_____

Saturday

How did it go today?   😕   😦   😐   🙂   😃

What successes did I enjoy today? *(Dig deep! Even small ones count, too!)*

_____

_____

What emerged/happened today that I want to work on, and what will I commit to doing?

_____

_____

Sunday

How did it go today?   😕   😦   😐   🙂   😃

What successes did I enjoy today? *(Dig deep! Even small ones count, too!)*

_____

_____

What emerged/happened today that I want to work on, and what will I commit to doing?

_____

_____

My week was:

_____

_____

_____

_____

_____

_____

WEEK 19

Remind yourself that if you think you already understand how someone feels or what they are trying to say, it is a delusion. Remember a time when you were sure you were right and then discovered one little fact that changed everything. There is always more to learn.

Douglas Stone (?) American author and Lecturer on Law at Harvard Law School

My initial reaction to this quotation is:

_____

_____

_____

Does the behavior embodied in this quotation show up in my relationships and/or my life? If so, how?

_____

_____

What positive changes will I make this week to incorporate this new insight into my behavior?

_____

_____

What obstacles can I see to implementing these positive changes?

_____

_____

What is my plan for overcoming these obstacles?

_____

_____

Monday

How did it go today?   🙁   😟   😐   🙂   😄

What successes did I enjoy today? *(Dig deep! Even small ones count, too!)*

_____

_____

What emerged/happened today that I want to work on, and what will I commit to doing?

_____

_____

Tuesday

How did it go today?   🙁   😟   😐   🙂   😄

What successes did I enjoy today? *(Dig deep! Even small ones count, too!)*

_____

_____

What emerged/happened today that I want to work on, and what will I commit to doing?

_____

_____

Wednesday

How did it go today?   🙁   😟   😐   🙂   😄

What successes did I enjoy today? *(Dig deep! Even small ones count, too!)*

_____

_____

What emerged/happened today that I want to work on, and what will I commit to doing?

_____

_____

Thursday

How did it go today?   🙁   😟   😐   🙂   😄

What successes did I enjoy today? *(Dig deep! Even small ones count, too!)*

_____

_____

What emerged/happened today that I want to work on, and what will I commit to doing?

_____

_____

Friday

How did it go today?

What successes did I enjoy today? *(Dig deep! Even small ones count, too!)*

_____

_____

What emerged/happened today that I want to work on, and what will I commit to doing?

_____

_____

Saturday

How did it go today?

What successes did I enjoy today? *(Dig deep! Even small ones count, too!)*

_____

_____

What emerged/happened today that I want to work on, and what will I commit to doing?

_____

_____

Sunday

How did it go today?

What successes did I enjoy today? *(Dig deep! Even small ones count, too!)*

_____

_____

What emerged/happened today that I want to work on, and what will I commit to doing?

_____

_____

My week was:

_____

_____

_____

_____

_____

_____

WEEK 20

To effectively communicate, we must realize that we are all different in the way we perceive the world and use this understanding as a guide to our communication with others.

Tony Robbins (1960–) American motivational speaker, personal finance instructor, and self-help author

My initial reaction to this quotation is:

_____

_____

_____

Does the behavior embodied in this quotation show up in my relationships and/or my life? If so, how?

_____

_____

What positive changes will I make this week to incorporate this new insight into my behavior?

_____

_____

What obstacles can I see to implementing these positive changes?

_____

_____

What is my plan for overcoming these obstacles?

_____

_____

Monday

How did it go today?

What successes did I enjoy today? *(Dig deep! Even small ones count, too!)*

_____

_____

What emerged/happened today that I want to work on, and what will I commit to doing?

_____

_____

Tuesday

How did it go today?

What successes did I enjoy today? *(Dig deep! Even small ones count, too!)*

_____

_____

What emerged/happened today that I want to work on, and what will I commit to doing?

_____

_____

Wednesday

How did it go today?

What successes did I enjoy today? *(Dig deep! Even small ones count, too!)*

_____

_____

What emerged/happened today that I want to work on, and what will I commit to doing?

_____

_____

Thursday

How did it go today?

What successes did I enjoy today? *(Dig deep! Even small ones count, too!)*

_____

_____

What emerged/happened today that I want to work on, and what will I commit to doing?

_____

_____

Friday

How did it go today?   😦 😦 😐 🙂 😀

What successes did I enjoy today? *(Dig deep! Even small ones count, too!)*

_____

_____

What emerged/happened today that I want to work on, and what will I commit to doing?

_____

_____

Saturday

How did it go today?   😦 😦 😐 🙂 😀

What successes did I enjoy today? *(Dig deep! Even small ones count, too!)*

_____

_____

What emerged/happened today that I want to work on, and what will I commit to doing?

_____

_____

Sunday

How did it go today?   😦 😦 😐 🙂 😀

What successes did I enjoy today? *(Dig deep! Even small ones count, too!)*

_____

_____

What emerged/happened today that I want to work on, and what will I commit to doing?

_____

_____

My week was:

_____

_____

_____

_____

_____

Extremists think "communication" means agreeing with them.

Leo Rosten (1908-1997) Polish-born American humorist, scriptwriter and journalist

My initial reaction to this quotation is:

_____

_____

_____

Does the behavior embodied in this quotation show up in my relationships and/or my life? If so, how?

_____

_____

What positive changes will I make this week to incorporate this new insight into my behavior?

_____

_____

What obstacles can I see to implementing these positive changes?

_____

_____

What is my plan for overcoming these obstacles?

_____

_____

Monday

How did it go today?   😦 ☹️ 😐 🙂 😃

What successes did I enjoy today? *(Dig deep! Even small ones count, too!)*

_____

_____

What emerged/happened today that I want to work on, and what will I commit to doing?

_____

Tuesday

How did it go today?   ☹️ ☹️ 😐 🙂 😃

What successes did I enjoy today? *(Dig deep! Even small ones count, too!)*

_____

_____

What emerged/happened today that I want to work on, and what will I commit to doing?

_____

_____

Wednesday

How did it go today?   ☹️ ☹️ 😐 🙂 😃

What successes did I enjoy today? *(Dig deep! Even small ones count, too!)*

_____

_____

What emerged/happened today that I want to work on, and what will I commit to doing?

_____

_____

Thursday

How did it go today?   ☹️ ☹️ 😐 🙂 😃

What successes did I enjoy today? *(Dig deep! Even small ones count, too!)*

_____

_____

What emerged/happened today that I want to work on, and what will I commit to doing?

_____

_____

Friday

How did it go today?

What successes did I enjoy today? *(Dig deep! Even small ones count, too!)*

_____

_____

What emerged/happened today that I want to work on, and what will I commit to doing?

_____

_____

Saturday

How did it go today?

What successes did I enjoy today? *(Dig deep! Even small ones count, too!)*

_____

_____

What emerged/happened today that I want to work on, and what will I commit to doing?

_____

_____

Sunday

How did it go today?

What successes did I enjoy today? *(Dig deep! Even small ones count, too!)*

_____

_____

What emerged/happened today that I want to work on, and what will I commit to doing?

_____

_____

My week was:

_____

_____

_____

_____

_____

_____

Every relationship has its problems. But if you're not willing to honestly express how you feel, how can you ever expect things to get better?

Stephan Labossiere (1978–) American certified relationship coach, speaker and author

My initial reaction to this quotation is:

_____

_____

_____

Does the behavior embodied in this quotation show up in my relationships and/or my life? If so, how?

_____

_____

What positive changes will I make this week to incorporate this new insight into my behavior?

_____

_____

What obstacles can I see to implementing these positive changes?

_____

_____

What is my plan for overcoming these obstacles?

_____

_____

Monday

How did it go today?   😦 😟 😐 🙂 😄

What successes did I enjoy today? *(Dig deep! Even small ones count, too!)*

_____

_____

What emerged/happened today that I want to work on, and what will I commit to doing?

_____

_____

Tuesday

How did it go today?   😦 😟 😐 🙂 😄

What successes did I enjoy today? *(Dig deep! Even small ones count, too!)*

_____

_____

What emerged/happened today that I want to work on, and what will I commit to doing?

_____

_____

Wednesday

How did it go today?   😦 😟 😐 🙂 😄

What successes did I enjoy today? *(Dig deep! Even small ones count, too!)*

_____

_____

What emerged/happened today that I want to work on, and what will I commit to doing?

_____

_____

Thursday

How did it go today?   😦 😟 😐 🙂 😄

What successes did I enjoy today? *(Dig deep! Even small ones count, too!)*

_____

_____

What emerged/happened today that I want to work on, and what will I commit to doing?

_____

_____

Friday

How did it go today?

What successes did I enjoy today? *(Dig deep! Even small ones count, too!)*

_____

_____

What emerged/happened today that I want to work on, and what will I commit to doing?

_____

_____

Saturday

How did it go today?

What successes did I enjoy today? *(Dig deep! Even small ones count, too!)*

_____

_____

What emerged/happened today that I want to work on, and what will I commit to doing?

_____

_____

Sunday

How did it go today?

What successes did I enjoy today? *(Dig deep! Even small ones count, too!)*

_____

_____

What emerged/happened today that I want to work on, and what will I commit to doing?

_____

_____

My week was:

_____

_____

_____

_____

_____

WEEK 23

Any problem, big or small, within a family, always seems to start with bad communication. Someone isn't listening.

Emma Thompson (1959-) British actress and screenwriter

My initial reaction to this quotation is:

_____

_____

_____

Does the behavior embodied in this quotation show up in my relationships and/or my life? If so, how?

_____

_____

What positive changes will I make this week to incorporate this new insight into my behavior?

_____

_____

What obstacles can I see to implementing these positive changes?

_____

_____

What is my plan for overcoming these obstacles?

_____

_____

Monday

How did it go today?

What successes did I enjoy today? *(Dig deep! Even small ones count, too!)*

_____

_____

What emerged/happened today that I want to work on, and what will I commit to doing?

_____

_____

Tuesday

How did it go today?

What successes did I enjoy today? *(Dig deep! Even small ones count, too!)*

_____

_____

What emerged/happened today that I want to work on, and what will I commit to doing?

_____

_____

Wednesday

How did it go today?

What successes did I enjoy today? *(Dig deep! Even small ones count, too!)*

_____

_____

What emerged/happened today that I want to work on, and what will I commit to doing?

_____

_____

Thursday

How did it go today?

What successes did I enjoy today? *(Dig deep! Even small ones count, too!)*

_____

_____

What emerged/happened today that I want to work on, and what will I commit to doing?

_____

_____

Friday

How did it go today?   😦 😦 😐 🙂 😃

What successes did I enjoy today? *(Dig deep! Even small ones count, too!)*

_____

_____

What emerged/happened today that I want to work on, and what will I commit to doing?

_____

_____

Saturday

How did it go today?   😦 😦 😐 🙂 😃

What successes did I enjoy today? *(Dig deep! Even small ones count, too!)*

_____

_____

What emerged/happened today that I want to work on, and what will I commit to doing?

_____

_____

Sunday

How did it go today?   😦 😦 😐 🙂 😃

What successes did I enjoy today? *(Dig deep! Even small ones count, too!)*

_____

_____

What emerged/happened today that I want to work on, and what will I commit to doing?

_____

_____

My week was:

_____

_____

_____

_____

_____

_____

Most people have to talk so they won't hear.

May Sarton (1912-1995), American poet, novelist and memoirist

My initial reaction to this quotation is:

_____

_____

_____

Does the behavior embodied in this quotation show up in my relationships and/or my life? If so, how?

_____

_____

What positive changes will I make this week to incorporate this new insight into my behavior?

_____

_____

What obstacles can I see to implementing these positive changes?

_____

_____

What is my plan for overcoming these obstacles?

_____

_____

Monday

How did it go today?   🙁 🙁 😐 🙂 😀

What successes did I enjoy today? *(Dig deep! Even small ones count, too!)*

_____

_____

What emerged/happened today that I want to work on, and what will I commit to doing?

_____

_____

Tuesday

How did it go today?   🙁 🙁 😐 🙂 😀

What successes did I enjoy today? *(Dig deep! Even small ones count, too!)*

_____

_____

What emerged/happened today that I want to work on, and what will I commit to doing?

_____

_____

Wednesday

How did it go today?   🙁 🙁 😐 🙂 😀

What successes did I enjoy today? *(Dig deep! Even small ones count, too!)*

_____

_____

What emerged/happened today that I want to work on, and what will I commit to doing?

_____

_____

Thursday

How did it go today?   🙁 🙁 😐 🙂 😀

What successes did I enjoy today? *(Dig deep! Even small ones count, too!)*

_____

_____

What emerged/happened today that I want to work on, and what will I commit to doing?

_____

_____

Friday

How did it go today?   🙁 🙁 😐 🙂 😀

What successes did I enjoy today? *(Dig deep! Even small ones count, too!)*

_____

_____

What emerged/happened today that I want to work on, and what will I commit to doing?

_____

_____

Saturday

How did it go today?   🙁 🙁 😐 🙂 😀

What successes did I enjoy today? *(Dig deep! Even small ones count, too!)*

_____

_____

What emerged/happened today that I want to work on, and what will I commit to doing?

_____

_____

Sunday

How did it go today?   🙁 🙁 😐 🙂 😀

What successes did I enjoy today? *(Dig deep! Even small ones count, too!)*

_____

_____

What emerged/happened today that I want to work on, and what will I commit to doing?

_____

_____

My week was:

_____

_____

_____

_____

_____

_____

Our lives begin to end the day we become silent about things that matter.

Martin Luther King, Jr. (1929-1968) American civil-rights activist and leader

My initial reaction to this quotation is:

_____
_____
_____

Does the behavior embodied in this quotation show up in my relationships and/or my life? If so, how?

_____
_____

What positive changes will I make this week to incorporate this new insight into my behavior?

_____
_____

What obstacles can I see to implementing these positive changes?

_____
_____

What is my plan for overcoming these obstacles?

_____
_____

Monday

How did it go today? 😞 😟 😐 🙂 😃

What successes did I enjoy today? *(Dig deep! Even small ones count, too!)*

_____

_____

What emerged/happened today that I want to work on, and what will I commit to doing?

_____

_____

Tuesday

How did it go today? 😞 😟 😐 🙂 😃

What successes did I enjoy today? *(Dig deep! Even small ones count, too!)*

_____

_____

What emerged/happened today that I want to work on, and what will I commit to doing?

_____

_____

Wednesday

How did it go today? 😞 😟 😐 🙂 😃

What successes did I enjoy today? *(Dig deep! Even small ones count, too!)*

_____

_____

What emerged/happened today that I want to work on, and what will I commit to doing?

_____

_____

Thursday

How did it go today? 😞 😟 😐 🙂 😃

What successes did I enjoy today? *(Dig deep! Even small ones count, too!)*

_____

_____

What emerged/happened today that I want to work on, and what will I commit to doing?

_____

_____

Friday

How did it go today?   😕   😦   😐   🙂   😃

What successes did I enjoy today? *(Dig deep! Even small ones count, too!)*

_____

_____

What emerged/happened today that I want to work on, and what will I commit to doing?

_____

_____

Saturday

How did it go today?   😕   😦   😐   🙂   😃

What successes did I enjoy today? *(Dig deep! Even small ones count, too!)*

_____

_____

What emerged/happened today that I want to work on, and what will I commit to doing?

_____

_____

Sunday

How did it go today?   😕   😦   😐   🙂   😃

What successes did I enjoy today? *(Dig deep! Even small ones count, too!)*

_____

_____

What emerged/happened today that I want to work on, and what will I commit to doing?

_____

_____

My week was:

_____

_____

_____

_____

_____

_____

Seek first to understand, then be understood.

Stephen Covey (1932-2012) American educator, author, businessman, and speaker

My initial reaction to this quotation is:

_____

_____

_____

Does the behavior embodied in this quotation show up in my relationships and/or my life? If so, how?

_____

_____

What positive changes will I make this week to incorporate this new insight into my behavior?

_____

_____

What obstacles can I see to implementing these positive changes?

_____

_____

What is my plan for overcoming these obstacles?

_____

_____

Monday

How did it go today? 🙁 😞 😐 🙂 😀

What successes did I enjoy today? *(Dig deep! Even small ones count, too!)*

_____

_____

What emerged/happened today that I want to work on, and what will I commit to doing?

_____

_____

Tuesday

How did it go today? 🙁 😞 😐 🙂 😀

What successes did I enjoy today? *(Dig deep! Even small ones count, too!)*

_____

_____

What emerged/happened today that I want to work on, and what will I commit to doing?

_____

_____

Wednesday

How did it go today? 🙁 😞 😐 🙂 😀

What successes did I enjoy today? *(Dig deep! Even small ones count, too!)*

_____

_____

What emerged/happened today that I want to work on, and what will I commit to doing?

_____

_____

Thursday

How did it go today? 🙁 😞 😐 🙂 😀

What successes did I enjoy today? *(Dig deep! Even small ones count, too!)*

_____

_____

What emerged/happened today that I want to work on, and what will I commit to doing?

_____

_____

Friday

How did it go today? 🙁 😕 😐 🙂 😀

What successes did I enjoy today? *(Dig deep! Even small ones count, too!)*

_____

_____

What emerged/happened today that I want to work on, and what will I commit to doing?

_____

_____

Saturday

How did it go today? 🙁 😕 😐 🙂 😀

What successes did I enjoy today? *(Dig deep! Even small ones count, too!)*

_____

_____

What emerged/happened today that I want to work on, and what will I commit to doing?

_____

_____

Sunday

How did it go today? 🙁 😕 😐 🙂 😀

What successes did I enjoy today? *(Dig deep! Even small ones count, too!)*

_____

_____

What emerged/happened today that I want to work on, and what will I commit to doing?

_____

_____

My week was:

_____

_____

_____

_____

_____

_____

Quarter 3:
The Third Pillar – *Mindful Reason*

Bringing mindfulness to processing everything you hear is an essential practice. Without it, you remain captive to emotional forces that can utterly undo you and your relationship. Engaging the power of your conscious mind, and taking full personal responsibility for your thoughts and actions, is the key to putting you in control of every situation.

Mindful Reason is my adaptation of the pioneering work of Dr. Albert Ellis, in combination with the recent application of timeless principles of mindfulness. Ellis created Rational Emotive Behavioral Therapy, the basis for much of the entire field of cognitive behavioral therapy. His contribution led to his peers voting him the second most influential psychologist of the 20th century, outscoring even Sigmund Freud!

Once you have set the stage for effective communication, you have to accept responsibility for what you do with the information you receive. *Mindful Reason* is the tool you can use to achieve that. For example, it comes in very handy when:

- You've been told something you find problematic at first blush
- You have something to say that you believe your partner may find problematic

- Your self-talk becomes problematic and is creating friction in your life and/or your relationship

By practicing *Mindful Reason*, you naturally increase your *Differentiation of Self*, which in turn leads to better relationships.

WEEK 27

How people treat you is their karma; how you react is yours.

Wayne Dyer, Ph.D. (1940-2015) American self-help author and motivational speaker

My initial reaction to this quotation is:

_____

_____

_____

Does the behavior embodied in this quotation show up in my relationships and/or my life? If so, how?

_____

_____

What positive changes will I make this week to incorporate this new insight into my behavior?

_____

_____

What obstacles can I see to implementing these positive changes?

_____

_____

What is my plan for overcoming these obstacles?

_____

_____

Monday

How did it go today? 😧 😟 😐 🙂 😃

What successes did I enjoy today? *(Dig deep! Even small ones count, too!)*

_____

_____

What emerged/happened today that I want to work on, and what will I commit to doing?

_____

_____

Tuesday

How did it go today? 😧 😟 😐 🙂 😃

What successes did I enjoy today? *(Dig deep! Even small ones count, too!)*

_____

_____

What emerged/happened today that I want to work on, and what will I commit to doing?

_____

_____

Wednesday

How did it go today? 😧 😟 😐 🙂 😃

What successes did I enjoy today? *(Dig deep! Even small ones count, too!)*

_____

_____

What emerged/happened today that I want to work on, and what will I commit to doing?

_____

_____

Thursday

How did it go today? 😧 😟 😐 🙂 😃

What successes did I enjoy today? *(Dig deep! Even small ones count, too!)*

_____

_____

What emerged/happened today that I want to work on, and what will I commit to doing?

_____

_____

Friday

How did it go today?   🙁 🙁 😐 🙂 😀

What successes did I enjoy today? *(Dig deep! Even small ones count, too!)*

_____

_____

What emerged/happened today that I want to work on, and what will I commit to doing?

_____

_____

Saturday

How did it go today?   🙁 🙁 😐 🙂 😀

What successes did I enjoy today? *(Dig deep! Even small ones count, too!)*

_____

_____

What emerged/happened today that I want to work on, and what will I commit to doing?

_____

_____

Sunday

How did it go today?   🙁 🙁 😐 🙂 😀

What successes did I enjoy today? *(Dig deep! Even small ones count, too!)*

_____

_____

What emerged/happened today that I want to work on, and what will I commit to doing?

_____

_____

My week was:

_____

_____

_____

_____

_____

_____

WEEK 28

You're only responsible for being honest, not for someone else's reaction to your honesty.

Kelli Jae Baeli (1962-) American bestselling novelist, independent publisher, editor, webmaster, blogger, artist, and singer-songwriter

My initial reaction to this quotation is:

_____

_____

_____

Does the behavior embodied in this quotation show up in my relationships and/or my life? If so, how?

_____

_____

What positive changes will I make this week to incorporate this new insight into my behavior?

_____

_____

What obstacles can I see to implementing these positive changes?

_____

_____

What is my plan for overcoming these obstacles?

_____

_____

Monday

How did it go today? 😦 🙁 😐 🙂 😄

What successes did I enjoy today? *(Dig deep! Even small ones count, too!)*

_____

_____

What emerged/happened today that I want to work on, and what will I commit to doing?

_____

_____

Tuesday

How did it go today? 😦 🙁 😐 🙂 😄

What successes did I enjoy today? *(Dig deep! Even small ones count, too!)*

_____

_____

What emerged/happened today that I want to work on, and what will I commit to doing?

_____

_____

Wednesday

How did it go today? 😦 🙁 😐 🙂 😄

What successes did I enjoy today? *(Dig deep! Even small ones count, too!)*

_____

_____

What emerged/happened today that I want to work on, and what will I commit to doing?

_____

_____

Thursday

How did it go today? 😦 🙁 😐 🙂 😄

What successes did I enjoy today? *(Dig deep! Even small ones count, too!)*

_____

_____

What emerged/happened today that I want to work on, and what will I commit to doing?

_____

_____

Friday

How did it go today?

What successes did I enjoy today? *(Dig deep! Even small ones count, too!)*

_____

_____

What emerged/happened today that I want to work on, and what will I commit to doing?

_____

_____

Saturday

How did it go today?

What successes did I enjoy today? *(Dig deep! Even small ones count, too!)*

_____

_____

What emerged/happened today that I want to work on, and what will I commit to doing?

_____

_____

Sunday

How did it go today?

What successes did I enjoy today? *(Dig deep! Even small ones count, too!)*

_____

_____

What emerged/happened today that I want to work on, and what will I commit to doing?

_____

_____

My week was:

_____

_____

_____

_____

_____

_____

When you say or do anything to please, get, keep, influence, or control anyone or anything, fear is the cause and pain is the result.

Byron Katie (1942-) American speaker and author

My initial reaction to this quotation is:

_____

_____

_____

Does the behavior embodied in this quotation show up in my relationships and/or my life? If so, how?

_____

_____

What positive changes will I make this week to incorporate this new insight into my behavior?

_____

_____

What obstacles can I see to implementing these positive changes?

_____

_____

What is my plan for overcoming these obstacles?

_____

_____

Monday

How did it go today?   😦 😟 😐 🙂 😄

What successes did I enjoy today? *(Dig deep! Even small ones count, too!)*

_____

_____

What emerged/happened today that I want to work on, and what will I commit to doing?

_____

_____

Tuesday

How did it go today?   😦 😟 😐 🙂 😄

What successes did I enjoy today? *(Dig deep! Even small ones count, too!)*

_____

_____

What emerged/happened today that I want to work on, and what will I commit to doing?

_____

_____

Wednesday

How did it go today?   😦 😟 😐 🙂 😄

What successes did I enjoy today? *(Dig deep! Even small ones count, too!)*

_____

_____

What emerged/happened today that I want to work on, and what will I commit to doing?

_____

_____

Thursday

How did it go today?   😦 😟 😐 🙂 😄

What successes did I enjoy today? *(Dig deep! Even small ones count, too!)*

_____

_____

What emerged/happened today that I want to work on, and what will I commit to doing?

_____

_____

Friday

How did it go today?

What successes did I enjoy today? *(Dig deep! Even small ones count, too!)*

_____
_____

What emerged/happened today that I want to work on, and what will I commit to doing?

_____
_____

Saturday

How did it go today?

What successes did I enjoy today? *(Dig deep! Even small ones count, too!)*

_____
_____

What emerged/happened today that I want to work on, and what will I commit to doing?

_____
_____

Sunday

How did it go today?

What successes did I enjoy today? *(Dig deep! Even small ones count, too!)*

_____
_____

What emerged/happened today that I want to work on, and what will I commit to doing?

_____
_____

My week was:

_____
_____
_____
_____
_____
_____

The only real security is not in owning or possessing, not in demanding or expecting, not in hoping, even. Security in a relationship lies neither in looking back to what it was, nor forward to what it might be, but living in the present and accepting it as it is now.

Anne Morrow Lindbergh (1906–2001) American author, aviator, and wife of fellow aviator Charles Lindbergh

My initial reaction to this quotation is:

_____

_____

_____

Does the behavior embodied in this quotation show up in my relationships and/or my life? If so, how?

_____

_____

What positive changes will I make this week to incorporate this new insight into my behavior?

_____

_____

What obstacles can I see to implementing these positive changes?

_____

_____

What is my plan for overcoming these obstacles?

_____

_____

Monday

How did it go today?   🙁 🙁 😐 🙂 😀

What successes did I enjoy today? *(Dig deep! Even small ones count, too!)*

_____

_____

What emerged/happened today that I want to work on, and what will I commit to doing?

_____

_____

Tuesday

How did it go today?   🙁 🙁 😐 🙂 😀

What successes did I enjoy today? *(Dig deep! Even small ones count, too!)*

_____

_____

What emerged/happened today that I want to work on, and what will I commit to doing?

_____

_____

Wednesday

How did it go today?   🙁 🙁 😐 🙂 😀

What successes did I enjoy today? *(Dig deep! Even small ones count, too!)*

_____

_____

What emerged/happened today that I want to work on, and what will I commit to doing?

_____

_____

Thursday

How did it go today?   🙁 🙁 😐 🙂 😀

What successes did I enjoy today? *(Dig deep! Even small ones count, too!)*

_____

_____

What emerged/happened today that I want to work on, and what will I commit to doing?

_____

_____

Friday

How did it go today?   😠 😞 😐 🙂 😃

What successes did I enjoy today? *(Dig deep! Even small ones count, too!)*

_____

_____

What emerged/happened today that I want to work on, and what will I commit to doing?

_____

_____

Saturday

How did it go today?   😠 😞 😐 🙂 😃

What successes did I enjoy today? *(Dig deep! Even small ones count, too!)*

_____

_____

What emerged/happened today that I want to work on, and what will I commit to doing?

_____

_____

Sunday

How did it go today?   😠 😞 😐 🙂 😃

What successes did I enjoy today? *(Dig deep! Even small ones count, too!)*

_____

_____

What emerged/happened today that I want to work on, and what will I commit to doing?

_____

_____

My week was:

_____

_____

_____

_____

_____

_____

WEEK 31

Begin challenging your own assumptions. Your assumptions are your windows on the world. Scrub them off every once in awhile, or the light won't come in.

Alan Alda (1936–) American actor, director, author and activist

My initial reaction to this quotation is:

_____

_____

_____

Does the behavior embodied in this quotation show up in my relationships and/or my life? If so, how?

_____

_____

What positive changes will I make this week to incorporate this new insight into my behavior?

_____

_____

What obstacles can I see to implementing these positive changes?

_____

_____

What is my plan for overcoming these obstacles?

_____

_____

Monday

How did it go today?   🙁 ☹️ 😐 🙂 😃

What successes did I enjoy today? *(Dig deep! Even small ones count, too!)*

_____

_____

What emerged/happened today that I want to work on, and what will I commit to doing?

_____

_____

Tuesday

How did it go today?   🙁 ☹️ 😐 🙂 😃

What successes did I enjoy today? *(Dig deep! Even small ones count, too!)*

_____

_____

What emerged/happened today that I want to work on, and what will I commit to doing?

_____

_____

Wednesday

How did it go today?   🙁 ☹️ 😐 🙂 😃

What successes did I enjoy today? *(Dig deep! Even small ones count, too!)*

_____

_____

What emerged/happened today that I want to work on, and what will I commit to doing?

_____

_____

Thursday

How did it go today?   🙁 ☹️ 😐 🙂 😃

What successes did I enjoy today? *(Dig deep! Even small ones count, too!)*

_____

_____

What emerged/happened today that I want to work on, and what will I commit to doing?

_____

_____

Friday

How did it go today? 😟 😦 😐 🙂 😃

What successes did I enjoy today? *(Dig deep! Even small ones count, too!)*

_____

_____

What emerged/happened today that I want to work on, and what will I commit to doing?

_____

_____

Saturday

How did it go today? 😟 😦 😐 🙂 😃

What successes did I enjoy today? *(Dig deep! Even small ones count, too!)*

_____

_____

What emerged/happened today that I want to work on, and what will I commit to doing?

_____

_____

Sunday

How did it go today? 😟 😦 😐 🙂 😃

What successes did I enjoy today? *(Dig deep! Even small ones count, too!)*

_____

_____

What emerged/happened today that I want to work on, and what will I commit to doing?

_____

_____

My week was:

_____

_____

_____

_____

_____

WEEK 32

Learning that you can't control the other person's reaction, and that it can be destructive to try, can be incredibly liberating. It not only gives the other person the space to react however they need to, but also takes a huge amount of pressure off you. You will learn things about yourself based on their reaction, but if you are prepared to learn, you'll feel free from the desperate need for their reaction to go one certain way.

Douglas Stone (?) American author, founder of Triad Consulting and a Lecturer on Law at Harvard Law School

My initial reaction to this quotation is:

_____

_____

_____

Does the behavior embodied in this quotation show up in my relationships and/or my life? If so, how?

_____

_____

What positive changes will I make this week to incorporate this new insight into my behavior?

_____

_____

What obstacles can I see to implementing these positive changes?

_____

_____

What is my plan for overcoming these obstacles?

_____

_____

Monday

How did it go today? 🙁 ☹️ 😐 🙂 😀

What successes did I enjoy today? *(Dig deep! Even small ones count, too!)*

_____

_____

What emerged/happened today that I want to work on, and what will I commit to doing?

_____

_____

Tuesday

How did it go today? 🙁 ☹️ 😐 🙂 😀

What successes did I enjoy today? *(Dig deep! Even small ones count, too!)*

_____

_____

What emerged/happened today that I want to work on, and what will I commit to doing?

_____

_____

Wednesday

How did it go today? 🙁 ☹️ 😐 🙂 😀

What successes did I enjoy today? *(Dig deep! Even small ones count, too!)*

_____

_____

What emerged/happened today that I want to work on, and what will I commit to doing?

_____

_____

Thursday

How did it go today? 🙁 ☹️ 😐 🙂 😀

What successes did I enjoy today? *(Dig deep! Even small ones count, too!)*

_____

_____

What emerged/happened today that I want to work on, and what will I commit to doing?

_____

_____

Friday

How did it go today?

What successes did I enjoy today? *(Dig deep! Even small ones count, too!)*

_____

_____

What emerged/happened today that I want to work on, and what will I commit to doing?

_____

_____

Saturday

How did it go today?

What successes did I enjoy today? *(Dig deep! Even small ones count, too!)*

_____

_____

What emerged/happened today that I want to work on, and what will I commit to doing?

_____

_____

Sunday

How did it go today?

What successes did I enjoy today? *(Dig deep! Even small ones count, too!)*

_____

_____

What emerged/happened today that I want to work on, and what will I commit to doing?

_____

_____

My week was:

_____

_____

_____

_____

_____

_____

WEEK 33

Mindfulness helps us freeze the frame so that we can become aware of our sensations and experiences as they are, without the distorting coloration of socially conditioned responses or habitual reactions.

Henepola Gunaratana (1927-) A Sri Lankan Theravada Buddhist monk

My initial reaction to this quotation is:

_____

_____

_____

Does the behavior embodied in this quotation show up in my relationships and/or my life? If so, how?

_____

_____

What positive changes will I make this week to incorporate this new insight into my behavior?

_____

_____

What obstacles can I see to implementing these positive changes?

_____

_____

What is my plan for overcoming these obstacles?

_____

_____

Monday

How did it go today?　　😟　😦　😐　🙂　😃

What successes did I enjoy today? *(Dig deep! Even small ones count, too!)*

_____

_____

What emerged/happened today that I want to work on, and what will I commit to doing?

_____

_____

Tuesday

How did it go today?　　😟　😦　😐　🙂　😃

What successes did I enjoy today? *(Dig deep! Even small ones count, too!)*

_____

_____

What emerged/happened today that I want to work on, and what will I commit to doing?

_____

_____

Wednesday

How did it go today?　　😟　😦　😐　🙂　😃

What successes did I enjoy today? *(Dig deep! Even small ones count, too!)*

_____

_____

What emerged/happened today that I want to work on, and what will I commit to doing?

_____

_____

Thursday

How did it go today?　　😟　😦　😐　🙂　😃

What successes did I enjoy today? *(Dig deep! Even small ones count, too!)*

_____

_____

What emerged/happened today that I want to work on, and what will I commit to doing?

_____

_____

Friday

How did it go today? 😞 😟 😐 🙂 😄

What successes did I enjoy today? *(Dig deep! Even small ones count, too!)*

_____

_____

What emerged/happened today that I want to work on, and what will I commit to doing?

_____

_____

Saturday

How did it go today? 😞 😟 😐 🙂 😄

What successes did I enjoy today? *(Dig deep! Even small ones count, too!)*

_____

_____

What emerged/happened today that I want to work on, and what will I commit to doing?

_____

_____

Sunday

How did it go today? 😞 😟 😐 🙂 😄

What successes did I enjoy today? *(Dig deep! Even small ones count, too!)*

_____

_____

What emerged/happened today that I want to work on, and what will I commit to doing?

_____

_____

My week was:

_____

_____

_____

_____

_____

When we direct our thoughts properly, we can control our emotions.

W. Clement Stone (1902-2002) American businessman, philanthropist and New Thought self-help book author

My initial reaction to this quotation is:

_____

_____

_____

Does the behavior embodied in this quotation show up in my relationships and/or my life? If so, how?

_____

_____

What positive changes will I make this week to incorporate this new insight into my behavior?

_____

_____

What obstacles can I see to implementing these positive changes?

_____

_____

What is my plan for overcoming these obstacles?

_____

_____

Monday

How did it go today? 😦 😖 😐 🙂 😃

What successes did I enjoy today? *(Dig deep! Even small ones count, too!)*

_____

_____

What emerged/happened today that I want to work on, and what will I commit to doing?

_____

Tuesday

How did it go today? 😦 😦 😐 🙂 😃

What successes did I enjoy today? *(Dig deep! Even small ones count, too!)*

_____

_____

What emerged/happened today that I want to work on, and what will I commit to doing?

_____

_____

Wednesday

How did it go today? 😦 😦 😐 🙂 😃

What successes did I enjoy today? *(Dig deep! Even small ones count, too!)*

_____

_____

What emerged/happened today that I want to work on, and what will I commit to doing?

_____

_____

Thursday

How did it go today? 😦 😦 😐 🙂 😃

What successes did I enjoy today? *(Dig deep! Even small ones count, too!)*

_____

_____

What emerged/happened today that I want to work on, and what will I commit to doing?

_____

_____

Friday

How did it go today? 😦 🙁 😐 🙂 😀

What successes did I enjoy today? *(Dig deep! Even small ones count, too!)*

_____

_____

What emerged/happened today that I want to work on, and what will I commit to doing?

_____

_____

Saturday

How did it go today? 😦 🙁 😐 🙂 😀

What successes did I enjoy today? *(Dig deep! Even small ones count, too!)*

_____

_____

What emerged/happened today that I want to work on, and what will I commit to doing?

_____

_____

Sunday

How did it go today? 😦 🙁 😐 🙂 😀

What successes did I enjoy today? *(Dig deep! Even small ones count, too!)*

_____

_____

What emerged/happened today that I want to work on, and what will I commit to doing?

_____

_____

My week was:

_____

_____

_____

_____

_____

_____

_____

WEEK 35

Every day we have plenty of opportunities to get angry, stressed or offended. But what you're doing when you indulge these negative emotions is giving something outside yourself power over your happiness. You can choose to not let little things upset you.

Joel Osteen (1963–) American minister, televangelist, author, and the Senior Pastor of Lakewood Church in Houston, Texas

My initial reaction to this quotation is:

_____

_____

_____

Does the behavior embodied in this quotation show up in my relationships and/or my life? If so, how?

_____

_____

What positive changes will I make this week to incorporate this new insight into my behavior?

_____

_____

What obstacles can I see to implementing these positive changes?

_____

_____

What is my plan for overcoming these obstacles?

_____

_____

Monday

How did it go today? 😦 😦 😐 🙂 😃

What successes did I enjoy today? *(Dig deep! Even small ones count, too!)*

_____

_____

What emerged/happened today that I want to work on, and what will I commit to doing?

_____

_____

Tuesday

How did it go today? 😦 😦 😐 🙂 😃

What successes did I enjoy today? *(Dig deep! Even small ones count, too!)*

_____

_____

What emerged/happened today that I want to work on, and what will I commit to doing?

_____

_____

Wednesday

How did it go today? 😦 😦 😐 🙂 😃

What successes did I enjoy today? *(Dig deep! Even small ones count, too!)*

_____

_____

What emerged/happened today that I want to work on, and what will I commit to doing?

_____

_____

Thursday

How did it go today? 😦 😦 😐 🙂 😃

What successes did I enjoy today? *(Dig deep! Even small ones count, too!)*

_____

_____

What emerged/happened today that I want to work on, and what will I commit to doing?

_____

_____

Friday

How did it go today?   🙁 ☹️ 😐 🙂 😀

What successes did I enjoy today? *(Dig deep! Even small ones count, too!)*

_____

_____

What emerged/happened today that I want to work on, and what will I commit to doing?

_____

_____

Saturday

How did it go today?   🙁 ☹️ 😐 🙂 😀

What successes did I enjoy today? *(Dig deep! Even small ones count, too!)*

_____

_____

What emerged/happened today that I want to work on, and what will I commit to doing?

_____

_____

Sunday

How did it go today?   🙁 ☹️ 😐 🙂 😀

What successes did I enjoy today? *(Dig deep! Even small ones count, too!)*

_____

_____

What emerged/happened today that I want to work on, and what will I commit to doing?

_____

_____

My week was:

_____

_____

_____

_____

_____

WEEK 36

Irrationally held truths may be more harmful than reasoned errors.

Thomas Henry Huxley (1825-1895) English biologist and anthropologist

My initial reaction to this quotation is:

_____

_____

_____

Does the behavior embodied in this quotation show up in my relationships and/or my life? If so, how?

_____

_____

What positive changes will I make this week to incorporate this new insight into my behavior?

_____

_____

What obstacles can I see to implementing these positive changes?

_____

_____

What is my plan for overcoming these obstacles?

_____

_____

Monday

How did it go today?

What successes did I enjoy today? *(Dig deep! Even small ones count, too!)*

_____

_____

What emerged/happened today that I want to work on, and what will I commit to doing?

_____

_____

Tuesday

How did it go today?

What successes did I enjoy today? *(Dig deep! Even small ones count, too!)*

_____

_____

What emerged/happened today that I want to work on, and what will I commit to doing?

_____

_____

Wednesday

How did it go today?

What successes did I enjoy today? *(Dig deep! Even small ones count, too!)*

_____

_____

What emerged/happened today that I want to work on, and what will I commit to doing?

_____

_____

Thursday

How did it go today?

What successes did I enjoy today? *(Dig deep! Even small ones count, too!)*

_____

_____

What emerged/happened today that I want to work on, and what will I commit to doing?

_____

_____

Friday

How did it go today? 😞 😟 😐 🙂 😃

What successes did I enjoy today? *(Dig deep! Even small ones count, too!)*

_____

_____

What emerged/happened today that I want to work on, and what will I commit to doing?

_____

_____

Saturday

How did it go today? 😞 😟 😐 🙂 😃

What successes did I enjoy today? *(Dig deep! Even small ones count, too!)*

_____

_____

What emerged/happened today that I want to work on, and what will I commit to doing?

_____

_____

Sunday

How did it go today? 😞 😟 😐 🙂 😃

What successes did I enjoy today? *(Dig deep! Even small ones count, too!)*

_____

_____

What emerged/happened today that I want to work on, and what will I commit to doing?

_____

_____

My week was:

_____

_____

_____

_____

_____

_____

If you don't like something, change it. If you can't change it, change your attitude.

Maya Angelou (1928-2014) American poet, author, and civil rights activist

My initial reaction to this quotation is:

_____

_____

_____

Does the behavior embodied in this quotation show up in my relationships and/or my life? If so, how?

_____

_____

What positive changes will I make this week to incorporate this new insight into my behavior?

_____

_____

What obstacles can I see to implementing these positive changes?

_____

_____

What is my plan for overcoming these obstacles?

_____

_____

Monday

How did it go today? 🙁 😕 😐 🙂 😃

What successes did I enjoy today? *(Dig deep! Even small ones count, too!)*

_____

_____

What emerged/happened today that I want to work on, and what will I commit to doing?

_____

_____

Tuesday

How did it go today? 🙁 😕 😐 🙂 😃

What successes did I enjoy today? *(Dig deep! Even small ones count, too!)*

_____

_____

What emerged/happened today that I want to work on, and what will I commit to doing?

_____

_____

Wednesday

How did it go today? 🙁 😕 😐 🙂 😃

What successes did I enjoy today? *(Dig deep! Even small ones count, too!)*

_____

_____

What emerged/happened today that I want to work on, and what will I commit to doing?

_____

_____

Thursday

How did it go today? 🙁 😕 😐 🙂 😃

What successes did I enjoy today? *(Dig deep! Even small ones count, too!)*

_____

_____

What emerged/happened today that I want to work on, and what will I commit to doing?

_____

_____

Friday

How did it go today? 😞 😦 😐 🙂 😀

What successes did I enjoy today? *(Dig deep! Even small ones count, too!)*

_____

_____

What emerged/happened today that I want to work on, and what will I commit to doing?

_____

_____

Saturday

How did it go today? 😞 😦 😐 🙂 😀

What successes did I enjoy today? *(Dig deep! Even small ones count, too!)*

_____

_____

What emerged/happened today that I want to work on, and what will I commit to doing?

_____

_____

Sunday

How did it go today? 😞 😦 😐 🙂 😀

What successes did I enjoy today? *(Dig deep! Even small ones count, too!)*

_____

_____

What emerged/happened today that I want to work on, and what will I commit to doing?

_____

_____

My week was:

_____

_____

_____

_____

_____

_____

WEEK 38

It is only possible to live happily ever after on a day-to-day basis.

Margaret Bonnano, (1950-2021) American writer and small press publisher

My initial reaction to this quotation is:

_____

_____

_____

Does the behavior embodied in this quotation show up in my relationships and/or my life? If so, how?

_____

_____

What positive changes will I make this week to incorporate this new insight into my behavior?

_____

_____

What obstacles can I see to implementing these positive changes?

_____

_____

What is my plan for overcoming these obstacles?

_____

_____

Monday

How did it go today?   🙁 😣 😐 🙂 😀

What successes did I enjoy today? *(Dig deep! Even small ones count, too!)*

_____

_____

What emerged/happened today that I want to work on, and what will I commit to doing?

_____

_____

Tuesday

How did it go today?   🙁 😣 😐 🙂 😀

What successes did I enjoy today? *(Dig deep! Even small ones count, too!)*

_____

_____

What emerged/happened today that I want to work on, and what will I commit to doing?

_____

_____

Wednesday

How did it go today?   🙁 😣 😐 🙂 😀

What successes did I enjoy today? *(Dig deep! Even small ones count, too!)*

_____

_____

What emerged/happened today that I want to work on, and what will I commit to doing?

_____

_____

Thursday

How did it go today?   🙁 😣 😐 🙂 😀

What successes did I enjoy today? *(Dig deep! Even small ones count, too!)*

_____

_____

What emerged/happened today that I want to work on, and what will I commit to doing?

_____

_____

Friday

How did it go today?

What successes did I enjoy today? *(Dig deep! Even small ones count, too!)*

_____

_____

What emerged/happened today that I want to work on, and what will I commit to doing?

_____

_____

Saturday

How did it go today?

What successes did I enjoy today? *(Dig deep! Even small ones count, too!)*

_____

_____

What emerged/happened today that I want to work on, and what will I commit to doing?

_____

_____

Sunday

How did it go today?

What successes did I enjoy today? *(Dig deep! Even small ones count, too!)*

_____

_____

What emerged/happened today that I want to work on, and what will I commit to doing?

_____

_____

My week was:

_____

_____

_____

_____

_____

_____

_____

WEEK 39

Freedom and happiness are won by disregarding things that lie beyond our control.

Epictetus (55-135 CE) A Greek-speaking Stoic philosopher, born in what is now Turkey

My initial reaction to this quotation is:

_____

_____

_____

Does the behavior embodied in this quotation show up in my relationships and/or my life? If so, how?

_____

_____

What positive changes will I make this week to incorporate this new insight into my behavior?

_____

_____

What obstacles can I see to implementing these positive changes?

_____

_____

What is my plan for overcoming these obstacles?

_____

_____

Monday

How did it go today?   😞 😟 😐 🙂 😀

What successes did I enjoy today? *(Dig deep! Even small ones count, too!)*

_____

_____

What emerged/happened today that I want to work on, and what will I commit to doing?

_____

_____

Tuesday

How did it go today?   😞 😟 😐 🙂 😀

What successes did I enjoy today? *(Dig deep! Even small ones count, too!)*

_____

_____

What emerged/happened today that I want to work on, and what will I commit to doing?

_____

_____

Wednesday

How did it go today?   😞 😟 😐 🙂 😀

What successes did I enjoy today? *(Dig deep! Even small ones count, too!)*

_____

_____

What emerged/happened today that I want to work on, and what will I commit to doing?

_____

_____

Thursday

How did it go today?   😞 😟 😐 🙂 😀

What successes did I enjoy today? *(Dig deep! Even small ones count, too!)*

_____

_____

What emerged/happened today that I want to work on, and what will I commit to doing?

_____

_____

Friday

How did it go today?

What successes did I enjoy today? *(Dig deep! Even small ones count, too!)*

_____

_____

What emerged/happened today that I want to work on, and what will I commit to doing?

_____

_____

Saturday

How did it go today?

What successes did I enjoy today? *(Dig deep! Even small ones count, too!)*

_____

_____

What emerged/happened today that I want to work on, and what will I commit to doing?

_____

_____

Sunday

How did it go today?

What successes did I enjoy today? *(Dig deep! Even small ones count, too!)*

_____

_____

What emerged/happened today that I want to work on, and what will I commit to doing?

_____

_____

My week was:

_____

_____

_____

_____

_____

_____

Quarter 4:
The Fourth Pillar –
Differentiation of Self

Being your authentic self (and expecting the same of your partner) is the key to a healthy and fulfilling relationship.

With respect to retaining personal responsibility and accountability while in relationship, I studied the work of psychiatrist Murray Bowen. Bowen developed his Family Systems Theory through decades of painstaking research. Psychologist David Schnarch then developed a method for using Bowen's principles in couples therapy. Bowen and Schnarch identified "differentiation of self" as critical to sustainable relationships. I felt that Albert Ellis' REBT — the inspiration for my *Mindful Reason* Pillar— was a perfect tool for improving one's differentiation of self. Melding Bowen's and Schnarch's insights with Ellis' discoveries gave me much of the basis for the *Differentiation of Self* Pillar of *Affirmative Intimacy*®.

Theologian Thomas F. Fischer, writing for pastors, defined differentiation of self as, "…a term used to describe one whose emotional process is no longer ultimately dependent on anything other than themselves. They are able to live and function on their own without undue anxiety or over-dependence on others. They are self-sufficient. Their sense of worth is not dependent on external relationships, circumstances or occurrences." I think this is as good a working definition as I've seen.

All important relationships generate a certain level of anxiety in us. The lack of differentiation of self shows up in intimate relationships as "emotional fusion" which can mean being too close to your partner and too sensitive to the emotional anxiety present in the relationship, or by "emotional cutoff," which is deliberate distancing within the relationship to avoid the anxiety. Neither is helpful. There is a robust body of research that demonstrates that the more differentiated the partners in a relationship are, the happier and more satisfying the relationship is perceived to be.

Once you gain the skills of co-creating *Safe Space*, using *Structured Dialog*, and viewing issues through the lens of *Mindful Reason*, your level of *Differentiation of Self* will certainly grow. To maximize that growth, I encourage you to focus specifically on applying these other tools consistently in your journey toward becoming a more independent, yet still fully present, participant in your relationship.

WEEK 40

Once the realization is accepted that even between the closest human beings infinite distances continue, a wonderful living side by side can grow, if they succeed in loving the distance between them which makes it possible for each to see the other whole against the sky.

Rainer Maria Rilke (1875-1926) Bohemian-Austrian poet and novelist

My initial reaction to this quotation is:

_____

_____

_____

Does the behavior embodied in this quotation show up in my relationships and/or my life? If so, how?

_____

_____

What positive changes will I make this week to incorporate this new insight into my behavior?

_____

_____

What obstacles can I see to implementing these positive changes?

_____

_____

What is my plan for overcoming these obstacles?

_____

_____

Monday

How did it go today? 🙁 🙁 😐 🙂 😄

What successes did I enjoy today? *(Dig deep! Even small ones count, too!)*

_____

_____

What emerged/happened today that I want to work on, and what will I commit to doing?

_____

_____

Tuesday

How did it go today? 🙁 🙁 😐 🙂 😄

What successes did I enjoy today? *(Dig deep! Even small ones count, too!)*

_____

_____

What emerged/happened today that I want to work on, and what will I commit to doing?

_____

_____

Wednesday

How did it go today? 🙁 🙁 😐 🙂 😄

What successes did I enjoy today? *(Dig deep! Even small ones count, too!)*

_____

_____

What emerged/happened today that I want to work on, and what will I commit to doing?

_____

_____

Thursday

How did it go today? 🙁 🙁 😐 🙂 😄

What successes did I enjoy today? *(Dig deep! Even small ones count, too!)*

_____

_____

What emerged/happened today that I want to work on, and what will I commit to doing?

_____

_____

Friday

How did it go today? 😦 😟 😐 🙂 😃

What successes did I enjoy today? *(Dig deep! Even small ones count, too!)*

_____

_____

What emerged/happened today that I want to work on, and what will I commit to doing?

_____

_____

Saturday

How did it go today? 😦 😟 😐 🙂 😃

What successes did I enjoy today? *(Dig deep! Even small ones count, too!)*

_____

_____

What emerged/happened today that I want to work on, and what will I commit to doing?

_____

_____

Sunday

How did it go today? 😦 😟 😐 🙂 😃

What successes did I enjoy today? *(Dig deep! Even small ones count, too!)*

_____

_____

What emerged/happened today that I want to work on, and what will I commit to doing?

_____

_____

My week was:

_____

_____

_____

_____

_____

The beginning of love is to let those we love be perfectly themselves, and not to twist them to fit our own image. Otherwise we love only the reflection of ourselves we find in them.

Thomas Merton (1915-1968) American Catholic writer, Trappist monk and mystic

My initial reaction to this quotation is:

_____

_____

_____

Does the behavior embodied in this quotation show up in my relationships and/or my life? If so, how?

_____

_____

What positive changes will I make this week to incorporate this new insight into my behavior?

_____

_____

What obstacles can I see to implementing these positive changes?

_____

_____

What is my plan for overcoming these obstacles?

_____

_____

Monday

How did it go today?

What successes did I enjoy today? *(Dig deep! Even small ones count, too!)*

_____

_____

What emerged/happened today that I want to work on, and what will I commit to doing?

_____

_____

Tuesday

How did it go today?

What successes did I enjoy today? *(Dig deep! Even small ones count, too!)*

_____

_____

What emerged/happened today that I want to work on, and what will I commit to doing?

_____

_____

Wednesday

How did it go today?

What successes did I enjoy today? *(Dig deep! Even small ones count, too!)*

_____

_____

What emerged/happened today that I want to work on, and what will I commit to doing?

_____

_____

Thursday

How did it go today?

What successes did I enjoy today? *(Dig deep! Even small ones count, too!)*

_____

_____

What emerged/happened today that I want to work on, and what will I commit to doing?

_____

_____

Friday

How did it go today?

What successes did I enjoy today? *(Dig deep! Even small ones count, too!)*

_____
_____

What emerged/happened today that I want to work on, and what will I commit to doing?

_____
_____

Saturday

How did it go today?

What successes did I enjoy today? *(Dig deep! Even small ones count, too!)*

_____
_____

What emerged/happened today that I want to work on, and what will I commit to doing?

_____
_____

Sunday

How did it go today?

What successes did I enjoy today? *(Dig deep! Even small ones count, too!)*

_____
_____

What emerged/happened today that I want to work on, and what will I commit to doing?

_____
_____

My week was:

_____
_____
_____
_____
_____
_____
_____

WEEK 42

> But let there be spaces in your togetherness and let the winds of the heavens dance between you. Love one another but make not a bond of love: let it rather be a moving sea between the shores of your souls.
>
> *Khalil Gibran (1883-1931) Lebanese-American artist, poet, and writer*

My initial reaction to this quotation is:

_____

_____

_____

Does the behavior embodied in this quotation show up in my relationships and/or my life? If so, how?

_____

_____

What positive changes will I make this week to incorporate this new insight into my behavior?

_____

_____

What obstacles can I see to implementing these positive changes?

_____

_____

What is my plan for overcoming these obstacles?

_____

_____

Monday

How did it go today?   😟 ☹️ 😐 🙂 😄

What successes did I enjoy today? *(Dig deep! Even small ones count, too!)*

_____

_____

What emerged/happened today that I want to work on, and what will I commit to doing?

_____

_____

Tuesday

How did it go today?   😟 ☹️ 😐 🙂 😄

What successes did I enjoy today? *(Dig deep! Even small ones count, too!)*

_____

_____

What emerged/happened today that I want to work on, and what will I commit to doing?

_____

_____

Wednesday

How did it go today?   😟 ☹️ 😐 🙂 😄

What successes did I enjoy today? *(Dig deep! Even small ones count, too!)*

_____

_____

What emerged/happened today that I want to work on, and what will I commit to doing?

_____

_____

Thursday

How did it go today?   😟 ☹️ 😐 🙂 😄

What successes did I enjoy today? *(Dig deep! Even small ones count, too!)*

_____

_____

What emerged/happened today that I want to work on, and what will I commit to doing?

_____

_____

Friday

How did it go today? 🙁 🙁 😐 🙂 😀

What successes did I enjoy today? *(Dig deep! Even small ones count, too!)*

_____

_____

What emerged/happened today that I want to work on, and what will I commit to doing?

_____

_____

Saturday

How did it go today? 🙁 🙁 😐 🙂 😀

What successes did I enjoy today? *(Dig deep! Even small ones count, too!)*

_____

_____

What emerged/happened today that I want to work on, and what will I commit to doing?

_____

_____

Sunday

How did it go today? 🙁 🙁 😐 🙂 😀

What successes did I enjoy today? *(Dig deep! Even small ones count, too!)*

_____

_____

What emerged/happened today that I want to work on, and what will I commit to doing?

_____

_____

My week was:

_____

_____

_____

_____

_____

WEEK 43

The concept of differentiation has to do with self and not with others. Differentiation deals with working on one's own self, with controlling self, with becoming a more responsible person, and permitting others to be themselves.

Murray Bowen, M.D. (1913-1990) American psychiatrist and professor, creator of the Family Systems psychiatric theory

My initial reaction to this quotation is:

_____

_____

_____

Does the behavior embodied in this quotation show up in my relationships and/or my life? If so, how?

_____

_____

What positive changes will I make this week to incorporate this new insight into my behavior?

_____

_____

What obstacles can I see to implementing these positive changes?

_____

_____

What is my plan for overcoming these obstacles?

_____

_____

Monday

How did it go today?   🙁 🙁 😐 🙂 😀

What successes did I enjoy today? *(Dig deep! Even small ones count, too!)*

_____

_____

What emerged/happened today that I want to work on, and what will I commit to doing?

_____

_____

Tuesday

How did it go today?   🙁 🙁 😐 🙂 😀

What successes did I enjoy today? *(Dig deep! Even small ones count, too!)*

_____

_____

What emerged/happened today that I want to work on, and what will I commit to doing?

_____

_____

Wednesday

How did it go today?   🙁 🙁 😐 🙂 😀

What successes did I enjoy today? *(Dig deep! Even small ones count, too!)*

_____

_____

What emerged/happened today that I want to work on, and what will I commit to doing?

_____

_____

Thursday

How did it go today?   🙁 🙁 😐 🙂 😀

What successes did I enjoy today? *(Dig deep! Even small ones count, too!)*

_____

_____

What emerged/happened today that I want to work on, and what will I commit to doing?

_____

_____

Friday

How did it go today?

What successes did I enjoy today? *(Dig deep! Even small ones count, too!)*

_____

_____

What emerged/happened today that I want to work on, and what will I commit to doing?

_____

_____

Saturday

How did it go today?

What successes did I enjoy today? *(Dig deep! Even small ones count, too!)*

_____

_____

What emerged/happened today that I want to work on, and what will I commit to doing?

_____

_____

Sunday

How did it go today?

What successes did I enjoy today? *(Dig deep! Even small ones count, too!)*

_____

_____

What emerged/happened today that I want to work on, and what will I commit to doing?

_____

_____

My week was:

_____

_____

_____

_____

_____

_____

WEEK 44

No partner in a love relationship...
should feel that he has to give up an
essential part of himself to make it
viable.

May Sarton (1912-1995), American poet, novelist and memoirist

My initial reaction to this quotation is:

_____
_____
_____

Does the behavior embodied in this quotation show up in my relationships and/or my life? If so, how?

_____
_____

What positive changes will I make this week to incorporate this new insight into my behavior?

_____
_____

What obstacles can I see to implementing these positive changes?

_____
_____

What is my plan for overcoming these obstacles?

_____
_____

Monday

How did it go today?   🙁 🙁 😐 🙂 😀

What successes did I enjoy today? *(Dig deep! Even small ones count, too!)*

_____

_____

What emerged/happened today that I want to work on, and what will I commit to doing?

_____

_____

Tuesday

How did it go today?   🙁 🙁 😐 🙂 😀

What successes did I enjoy today? *(Dig deep! Even small ones count, too!)*

_____

_____

What emerged/happened today that I want to work on, and what will I commit to doing?

_____

_____

Wednesday

How did it go today?   🙁 🙁 😐 🙂 😀

What successes did I enjoy today? *(Dig deep! Even small ones count, too!)*

_____

_____

What emerged/happened today that I want to work on, and what will I commit to doing?

_____

_____

Thursday

How did it go today?   🙁 🙁 😐 🙂 😀

What successes did I enjoy today? *(Dig deep! Even small ones count, too!)*

_____

_____

What emerged/happened today that I want to work on, and what will I commit to doing?

_____

_____

Friday

How did it go today? 😟 😦 😐 🙂 😃

What successes did I enjoy today? *(Dig deep! Even small ones count, too!)*

_____

_____

What emerged/happened today that I want to work on, and what will I commit to doing?

_____

_____

Saturday

How did it go today? 😟 😦 😐 🙂 😃

What successes did I enjoy today? *(Dig deep! Even small ones count, too!)*

_____

_____

What emerged/happened today that I want to work on, and what will I commit to doing?

_____

_____

Sunday

How did it go today? 😟 😦 😐 🙂 😃

What successes did I enjoy today? *(Dig deep! Even small ones count, too!)*

_____

_____

What emerged/happened today that I want to work on, and what will I commit to doing?

_____

_____

My week was:

_____

_____

_____

_____

_____

_____

WEEK 45

There are days when you need someone who just wants to be your sunshine and not the air you breathe.

Robert Brault (1938-) American freelance writer and author

My initial reaction to this quotation is:

_____

_____

_____

Does the behavior embodied in this quotation show up in my relationships and/or my life? If so, how?

_____

_____

What positive changes will I make this week to incorporate this new insight into my behavior?

_____

_____

What obstacles can I see to implementing these positive changes?

_____

_____

What is my plan for overcoming these obstacles?

_____

_____

Monday

How did it go today?   🙁 🙁 😐 🙂 😃

What successes did I enjoy today? *(Dig deep! Even small ones count, too!)*

_____

_____

What emerged/happened today that I want to work on, and what will I commit to doing?

_____

_____

Tuesday

How did it go today?   🙁 🙁 😐 🙂 😃

What successes did I enjoy today? *(Dig deep! Even small ones count, too!)*

_____

_____

What emerged/happened today that I want to work on, and what will I commit to doing?

_____

_____

Wednesday

How did it go today?   🙁 🙁 😐 🙂 😃

What successes did I enjoy today? *(Dig deep! Even small ones count, too!)*

_____

_____

What emerged/happened today that I want to work on, and what will I commit to doing?

_____

_____

Thursday

How did it go today?   🙁 🙁 😐 🙂 😃

What successes did I enjoy today? *(Dig deep! Even small ones count, too!)*

_____

_____

What emerged/happened today that I want to work on, and what will I commit to doing?

_____

_____

Friday

How did it go today?   🙁 😟 😐 🙂 😀

What successes did I enjoy today? *(Dig deep! Even small ones count, too!)*

_____

_____

What emerged/happened today that I want to work on, and what will I commit to doing?

_____

_____

Saturday

How did it go today?   🙁 😟 😐 🙂 😀

What successes did I enjoy today? *(Dig deep! Even small ones count, too!)*

_____

_____

What emerged/happened today that I want to work on, and what will I commit to doing?

_____

_____

Sunday

How did it go today?   🙁 😟 😐 🙂 😀

What successes did I enjoy today? *(Dig deep! Even small ones count, too!)*

_____

_____

What emerged/happened today that I want to work on, and what will I commit to doing?

_____

_____

My week was:

_____

_____

_____

_____

_____

_____

Differentiation is your ability to maintain your sense of self when you are emotionally and/or physically close to others — especially as they become increasingly important to you.

David Schnarch, Ph.D. (1946-2020) American licensed clinical psychologist and author

My initial reaction to this quotation is:

_____

_____

_____

Does the behavior embodied in this quotation show up in my relationships and/or my life? If so, how?

_____

_____

What positive changes will I make this week to incorporate this new insight into my behavior?

_____

_____

What obstacles can I see to implementing these positive changes?

_____

_____

What is my plan for overcoming these obstacles?

_____

_____

Monday

How did it go today?   😞 😟 😐 🙂 😄

What successes did I enjoy today? *(Dig deep! Even small ones count, too!)*

_____

_____

What emerged/happened today that I want to work on, and what will I commit to doing?

_____

_____

Tuesday

How did it go today?   😞 😟 😐 🙂 😄

What successes did I enjoy today? *(Dig deep! Even small ones count, too!)*

_____

_____

What emerged/happened today that I want to work on, and what will I commit to doing?

_____

_____

Wednesday

How did it go today?   😞 😟 😐 🙂 😄

What successes did I enjoy today? *(Dig deep! Even small ones count, too!)*

_____

_____

What emerged/happened today that I want to work on, and what will I commit to doing?

_____

_____

Thursday

How did it go today?   😞 😟 😐 🙂 😄

What successes did I enjoy today? *(Dig deep! Even small ones count, too!)*

_____

_____

What emerged/happened today that I want to work on, and what will I commit to doing?

_____

_____

Friday

How did it go today?   🙁 🙁 😐 🙂 😃

What successes did I enjoy today? *(Dig deep! Even small ones count, too!)*

_____

_____

What emerged/happened today that I want to work on, and what will I commit to doing?

_____

_____

Saturday

How did it go today?   🙁 🙁 😐 🙂 😃

What successes did I enjoy today? *(Dig deep! Even small ones count, too!)*

_____

_____

What emerged/happened today that I want to work on, and what will I commit to doing?

_____

_____

Sunday

How did it go today?   🙁 🙁 😐 🙂 😃

What successes did I enjoy today? *(Dig deep! Even small ones count, too!)*

_____

_____

What emerged/happened today that I want to work on, and what will I commit to doing?

_____

_____

My week was:

_____

_____

_____

_____

_____

WEEK 47

[R]elationship work, paradoxically, is a solitary project...It is not necessary, important, or even possible to work on the other person. One cannot change another person, though the temptation to try is always there. Change must come from within the self, for one's own reasons.

Roberta M. Gilbert, M.D. (?) American psychiatrist whose special interest is Bowen Family Systems theory

My initial reaction to this quotation is:

_____

_____

_____

Does the behavior embodied in this quotation show up in my relationships and/or my life? If so, how?

_____

_____

What positive changes will I make this week to incorporate this new insight into my behavior?

_____

_____

What obstacles can I see to implementing these positive changes?

_____

_____

What is my plan for overcoming these obstacles?

_____

_____

Monday

How did it go today?   😦 😕 😐 🙂 😄

What successes did I enjoy today? *(Dig deep! Even small ones count, too!)*

_____

_____

What emerged/happened today that I want to work on, and what will I commit to doing?

_____

_____

Tuesday

How did it go today?   😦 😦 😐 🙂 😄

What successes did I enjoy today? *(Dig deep! Even small ones count, too!)*

_____

_____

What emerged/happened today that I want to work on, and what will I commit to doing?

_____

_____

Wednesday

How did it go today?   😦 😦 😐 🙂 😄

What successes did I enjoy today? *(Dig deep! Even small ones count, too!)*

_____

_____

What emerged/happened today that I want to work on, and what will I commit to doing?

_____

_____

Thursday

How did it go today?   😦 😦 😐 🙂 😄

What successes did I enjoy today? *(Dig deep! Even small ones count, too!)*

_____

_____

What emerged/happened today that I want to work on, and what will I commit to doing?

_____

_____

Friday

How did it go today?

What successes did I enjoy today? *(Dig deep! Even small ones count, too!)*

_____

_____

What emerged/happened today that I want to work on, and what will I commit to doing?

_____

_____

Saturday

How did it go today?

What successes did I enjoy today? *(Dig deep! Even small ones count, too!)*

_____

_____

What emerged/happened today that I want to work on, and what will I commit to doing?

_____

_____

Sunday

How did it go today?

What successes did I enjoy today? *(Dig deep! Even small ones count, too!)*

_____

_____

What emerged/happened today that I want to work on, and what will I commit to doing?

_____

_____

My week was:

_____

_____

_____

_____

_____

_____

WEEK 48

Care about what other people think
and you will always be their prisoner.

Lao Tzu (?-531 BCE) A philosopher and poet of ancient China.
He is known as the reputed author of the Tao Te Ching and the
founder of philosophical Taoism

My initial reaction to this quotation is:

_____
_____
_____

Does the behavior embodied in this quotation show up in my relationships and/or my life? If so, how?

_____
_____

What positive changes will I make this week to incorporate this new insight into my behavior?

_____
_____

What obstacles can I see to implementing these positive changes?

_____
_____

What is my plan for overcoming these obstacles?

_____
_____

Monday

How did it go today? 😦 😟 😐 🙂 😄

What successes did I enjoy today? *(Dig deep! Even small ones count, too!)*

_____

_____

What emerged/happened today that I want to work on, and what will I commit to doing?

_____

_____

Tuesday

How did it go today? 😦 😟 😐 🙂 😄

What successes did I enjoy today? *(Dig deep! Even small ones count, too!)*

_____

_____

What emerged/happened today that I want to work on, and what will I commit to doing?

_____

_____

Wednesday

How did it go today? 😦 😟 😐 🙂 😄

What successes did I enjoy today? *(Dig deep! Even small ones count, too!)*

_____

_____

What emerged/happened today that I want to work on, and what will I commit to doing?

_____

_____

Thursday

How did it go today? 😦 😟 😐 🙂 😄

What successes did I enjoy today? *(Dig deep! Even small ones count, too!)*

_____

_____

What emerged/happened today that I want to work on, and what will I commit to doing?

_____

_____

Friday

How did it go today?

What successes did I enjoy today? *(Dig deep! Even small ones count, too!)*

_____

_____

What emerged/happened today that I want to work on, and what will I commit to doing?

_____

_____

Saturday

How did it go today?

What successes did I enjoy today? *(Dig deep! Even small ones count, too!)*

_____

_____

What emerged/happened today that I want to work on, and what will I commit to doing?

_____

_____

Sunday

How did it go today?

What successes did I enjoy today? *(Dig deep! Even small ones count, too!)*

_____

_____

What emerged/happened today that I want to work on, and what will I commit to doing?

_____

_____

My week was:

_____

_____

_____

_____

_____

_____

WEEK 49

Love is the ability and willingness to allow those that you care for to be what they choose for themselves without any insistence that they satisfy you.

Wayne Dyer, Ph.D. (1940–2015) American self-help author and motivational speaker

My initial reaction to this quotation is:

_____

_____

_____

Does the behavior embodied in this quotation show up in my relationships and/or my life? If so, how?

_____

_____

What positive changes will I make this week to incorporate this new insight into my behavior?

_____

_____

What obstacles can I see to implementing these positive changes?

_____

_____

What is my plan for overcoming these obstacles?

_____

_____

Monday

How did it go today?

What successes did I enjoy today? *(Dig deep! Even small ones count, too!)*

_____

_____

What emerged/happened today that I want to work on, and what will I commit to doing?

_____

_____

Tuesday

How did it go today?

What successes did I enjoy today? *(Dig deep! Even small ones count, too!)*

_____

_____

What emerged/happened today that I want to work on, and what will I commit to doing?

_____

_____

Wednesday

How did it go today?

What successes did I enjoy today? *(Dig deep! Even small ones count, too!)*

_____

_____

What emerged/happened today that I want to work on, and what will I commit to doing?

_____

_____

Thursday

How did it go today?

What successes did I enjoy today? *(Dig deep! Even small ones count, too!)*

_____

_____

What emerged/happened today that I want to work on, and what will I commit to doing?

_____

_____

Friday

How did it go today? 😞 😟 😐 🙂 😄

What successes did I enjoy today? *(Dig deep! Even small ones count, too!)*

_____
_____

What emerged/happened today that I want to work on, and what will I commit to doing?

_____
_____

Saturday

How did it go today? 😞 😟 😐 🙂 😄

What successes did I enjoy today? *(Dig deep! Even small ones count, too!)*

_____
_____

What emerged/happened today that I want to work on, and what will I commit to doing?

_____
_____

Sunday

How did it go today? 😞 😟 😐 🙂 😄

What successes did I enjoy today? *(Dig deep! Even small ones count, too!)*

_____
_____

What emerged/happened today that I want to work on, and what will I commit to doing?

_____
_____

My week was:

_____
_____
_____
_____
_____
_____

Jealousy: A form of emotional fusion. At its most severe, jealousy illustrates our intolerance for boundaries and separateness from those we love.

David Schnarch, Ph.D. (1946–2020) American licensed clinical psychologist and author

My initial reaction to this quotation is:

_____

_____

_____

Does the behavior embodied in this quotation show up in my relationships and/or my life? If so, how?

_____

_____

What positive changes will I make this week to incorporate this new insight into my behavior?

_____

_____

What obstacles can I see to implementing these positive changes?

_____

_____

What is my plan for overcoming these obstacles?

_____

_____

Monday

How did it go today? 😞 😟 😐 🙂 😀

What successes did I enjoy today? *(Dig deep! Even small ones count, too!)*

_____

_____

What emerged/happened today that I want to work on, and what will I commit to doing?

_____

_____

Tuesday

How did it go today? 😞 😟 😐 🙂 😀

What successes did I enjoy today? *(Dig deep! Even small ones count, too!)*

_____

_____

What emerged/happened today that I want to work on, and what will I commit to doing?

_____

_____

Wednesday

How did it go today? 😞 😟 😐 🙂 😀

What successes did I enjoy today? *(Dig deep! Even small ones count, too!)*

_____

_____

What emerged/happened today that I want to work on, and what will I commit to doing?

_____

_____

Thursday

How did it go today? 😞 😟 😐 🙂 😀

What successes did I enjoy today? *(Dig deep! Even small ones count, too!)*

_____

_____

What emerged/happened today that I want to work on, and what will I commit to doing?

_____

_____

Friday

How did it go today?

What successes did I enjoy today? *(Dig deep! Even small ones count, too!)*

_____

_____

What emerged/happened today that I want to work on, and what will I commit to doing?

_____

_____

Saturday

How did it go today?

What successes did I enjoy today? *(Dig deep! Even small ones count, too!)*

_____

_____

What emerged/happened today that I want to work on, and what will I commit to doing?

_____

_____

Sunday

How did it go today?

What successes did I enjoy today? *(Dig deep! Even small ones count, too!)*

_____

_____

What emerged/happened today that I want to work on, and what will I commit to doing?

_____

_____

My week was:

_____

_____

_____

_____

_____

WEEK 51

The most painful thing is losing yourself in the process of loving someone too much, and forgetting that you are special too.

Ernest Hemingway (1899-1961) American novelist, short-story writer, and journalist

My initial reaction to this quotation is:

_____

_____

_____

Does the behavior embodied in this quotation show up in my relationships and/or my life? If so, how?

_____

_____

What positive changes will I make this week to incorporate this new insight into my behavior?

_____

_____

What obstacles can I see to implementing these positive changes?

_____

_____

What is my plan for overcoming these obstacles?

_____

_____

Monday

How did it go today? 😞 😟 😐 🙂 😄

What successes did I enjoy today? *(Dig deep! Even small ones count, too!)*

_____

_____

What emerged/happened today that I want to work on, and what will I commit to doing?

_____

_____

Tuesday

How did it go today? 😞 😟 😐 🙂 😄

What successes did I enjoy today? *(Dig deep! Even small ones count, too!)*

_____

_____

What emerged/happened today that I want to work on, and what will I commit to doing?

_____

_____

Wednesday

How did it go today? 😞 😟 😐 🙂 😄

What successes did I enjoy today? *(Dig deep! Even small ones count, too!)*

_____

_____

What emerged/happened today that I want to work on, and what will I commit to doing?

_____

_____

Thursday

How did it go today? 😞 😟 😐 🙂 😄

What successes did I enjoy today? *(Dig deep! Even small ones count, too!)*

_____

_____

What emerged/happened today that I want to work on, and what will I commit to doing?

_____

_____

Friday

How did it go today?

What successes did I enjoy today? *(Dig deep! Even small ones count, too!)*

_____

_____

What emerged/happened today that I want to work on, and what will I commit to doing?

_____

_____

Saturday

How did it go today?

What successes did I enjoy today? *(Dig deep! Even small ones count, too!)*

_____

_____

What emerged/happened today that I want to work on, and what will I commit to doing?

_____

_____

Sunday

How did it go today?

What successes did I enjoy today? *(Dig deep! Even small ones count, too!)*

_____

_____

What emerged/happened today that I want to work on, and what will I commit to doing?

_____

_____

My week was:

_____

_____

_____

_____

_____

_____

WEEK 52

Remember always that you not only have the right to be an individual, you have an obligation to be one.

Eleanor Roosevelt (1884-1962) American political figure, diplomat, and activist

My initial reaction to this quotation is:

_____

_____

_____

Does the behavior embodied in this quotation show up in my relationships and/or my life? If so, how?

_____

_____

What positive changes will I make this week to incorporate this new insight into my behavior?

_____

_____

What obstacles can I see to implementing these positive changes?

_____

_____

What is my plan for overcoming these obstacles?

_____

_____

Monday

How did it go today?   😦 😧 😐 🙂 😀

What successes did I enjoy today? *(Dig deep! Even small ones count, too!)*

_____

_____

What emerged/happened today that I want to work on, and what will I commit to doing?

_____

_____

Tuesday

How did it go today?   😦 😧 😐 🙂 😀

What successes did I enjoy today? *(Dig deep! Even small ones count, too!)*

_____

_____

What emerged/happened today that I want to work on, and what will I commit to doing?

_____

_____

Wednesday

How did it go today?   😦 😧 😐 🙂 😀

What successes did I enjoy today? *(Dig deep! Even small ones count, too!)*

_____

_____

What emerged/happened today that I want to work on, and what will I commit to doing?

_____

_____

Thursday

How did it go today?   😦 😧 😐 🙂 😀

What successes did I enjoy today? *(Dig deep! Even small ones count, too!)*

_____

_____

What emerged/happened today that I want to work on, and what will I commit to doing?

_____

_____

Friday

How did it go today?

What successes did I enjoy today? *(Dig deep! Even small ones count, too!)*

_____

_____

What emerged/happened today that I want to work on, and what will I commit to doing?

_____

_____

Saturday

How did it go today?

What successes did I enjoy today? *(Dig deep! Even small ones count, too!)*

_____

_____

What emerged/happened today that I want to work on, and what will I commit to doing?

_____

_____

Sunday

How did it go today?

What successes did I enjoy today? *(Dig deep! Even small ones count, too!)*

_____

_____

What emerged/happened today that I want to work on, and what will I commit to doing?

_____

_____

My week was:

_____

_____

_____

_____

_____

James R. Fleckenstein

Jim Fleckenstein became a relationship coach and educator because of his life experiences. When his 25-year marriage ended, he combined the skills he'd gained from his prior successful non-profit career with his insatiable curiosity to learn about creating better relationships. He founded an educational non-profit to foster new research into relationships. He also began rigorous self-education, including reaching out personally to leading researchers.

His efforts quickly bore fruit. His organization ultimately conducted five national conferences on relationships. He merged this organization into another group in 2006. This let him focus on education, research, and helping people have successful relationships.

Jim was invited to co-present to a professional audience for the first time in 2002. He spoke to the American Association of Sexuality Educators, Counselors and Therapists (AASECT). He has since been invited to present at seven more AASECT conferences. He's also presented at:

- The Society for the Scientific Study of Sexuality
- The Society for Sex Therapy and Research
- The American Association for Marriage and Family Therapy

Jim was an invited contributor to the *Continuum Complete International Encyclopedia of Sexuality* in 2004. In 2015, he published his first research paper in the peer-reviewed journal *Sexual and Relationship Therapy*. This paper became a chapter in the 2015 book, *Sexuality and Aging*. His second research paper appeared in *The Archives of Sexual Behavior* in 2021. Since 2016, he has served as Production Editor of *The Journal of Positive Sexuality*. Jim is also a regular presenter at lay conferences, reaching hundreds.

Jim developed a unique approach to relationships based on proven methods he encountered over his years of study. He formalized this approach as his *Affirmative Intimacy*® method. Jim created The Earth Moved, LLC in 2012 as a home for his coaching and educational efforts. His first book, *Love That Works: 38 Awesome Hacks for Amazing Relationships*, appeared in 2019.

Jim lives in Virginia with his partner, the novelist Solara Gordon.

One final thought...

There are limits to what you can accomplish by yourself. Your personal commitment to building a better intimate relationship is essential. But that alone won't bring you maximum success. This journal, and my associated book, *Love That Works: 38 Awesome Hacks for Amazing Relationships*, are powerful tools. If you apply them, you *will* see progress. You may even get to a place where you're satisfied.

But even if you do – *and I assure you, most people reading this won't* – it will take you longer and be harder than it needs to.

Self-help is awesome. It sets the stage for growth and progress. I absolutely believe in it. I've used it myself to good advantage.

But it seldom gets you to the finish line.

There's a powerful saying that I find applies to many situations, and this is no exception.

You can have it good, cheap, or fast. Pick any two.

What combination do *you* want to stake the success of your intimate relationship on?

- Do you want to spend years trying to figure this out on your own, by trial and error? (= cheap, good (maybe), not fast)

- Do you want to keep buying self-help books and relying on "Dr. Google"? (= fast, cheap (maybe), not good)

- Do you want personalized help in navigating the rough spots and putting this new-found knowledge to work? Do you want to *have* the relationship you *deserve*? (= fast, good, not cheap (maybe))

I know which option I'd choose.

You may want to explore working with me personally to apply what you're learning here and in *Love That Works: 38 Awesome Hacks for Amazing Relationships*. In that case, I invite you to reach out to me. There's no cost to have this chat.

Follow this link: https://calendly.com/affirmativeintimacy/ice-call

www.ingramcontent.com/pod-product-compliance
Lightning Source LLC
Chambersburg PA
CBHW052330100426
42737CB00055B/3305